The Unauthorized History of

DALLAS, TEXAS

By

Rose-Mary Rumbley, Ph.D.

Enjoy Big D —
Rose-mary Rumbley

EAKIN PRESS ★ Austin, Texas

Contents

iv

Acknowledgments

Dedicated to John Patton, who was a fine newspaperman who encouraged me to write my column for the *Oak Cliff Tribune,* and to Donnie Gililland, a fine musician and writer who wrote most of the chapter headings in this book.

A big thanks to my family, my husband, Jack, my son, Phil, his wife, Karen, and little Scotty, and my daughter, Jill, and her husband, Ken Beam, and the kids, Daulton and Cassandra.

Also a big thanks to Mr. Ed Eakin, publisher, who has always believed me when I said, "This is a great book!"

Also a big thanks to the staff at the *Oak Cliff Tribune* who has continued to publish my column.

And too, a big thanks to the gang on the seventh floor, Dallas Public Library.

CHAPTER I

Some of Mother's Stories

MY ROOTS

After English and Prussian troops defeated Napoleon in 1815, the British people went on to bigger and better things. However, the Prussians and the Germans did not prosper as a whole. Some did, but the majority did not do well at all. There were several reasons for the discontent and misery amid the German people.

Steam had replaced the old fuels that were still being used in the industries of Germany. Also, the country had no port on the Atlantic which had become the waterway of the world. Feudal laws still existed, so these industrious people were trapped into poverty and stagnation. They were looking for a way out and it came in 1820, when Stephen F. Austin made the deal with the Mexican government to colonize Texas. A person could come in and claim the fine land offered in this southern section of North America.

Word about this deal got to Germany, and the people came. One German prince came and led his people into the best land of the whole area — the Hill Country. This prince was Carl of Solms-Braunfels, and he and his bunch built the little city, New Braunfels. His city soon became one of the largest cities in Texas because of the

1

ideal climate and abundant natural resources. Agriculture and industry thrived.

The Germans could do anything — they were butchers, blacksmiths, bakers, cabinetmakers, coppersmiths, locksmiths, machinists, saddlers, tailors, shoemakers, tanners. They were ever so grateful for the new beginning and they cashed in on it. They became truly tough Texans who triumphed over epidemics and all sorts of hardships. Later, they even fought with Sam Houston for the Republic and they fought in the Civil War for the South.

My daddy's family, the Braus and the Etzels, came from Germany in the midst of this Texas migration. They settled in Round Top, Fayette County, and prospered by raising cotton in the rich soil of the Hill Country. My mother's family on her mother's side, the Balitzs, wandered all the way up to Dallas after the Civil War. They had four daughters, Rosalie, my grandmother, Emma, Pauline, and Elsie. My mother's father, William Hass, appeared on the Dallas scene in the 1880s. We're not sure from whence he came. He just popped up in Dallas with his half brother, Frank Gerlach. They were German. Frank settled in the little town of Lisbon and opened a blacksmith shop. Later, he moved his shop to Main Street, Dallas. William opened the West End Bakery in the heart of Downtown Dallas. The brothers married Balitz girls. William married Rosalie, and Frank married Emma.

MY MOTHER LIVED DOWNTOWN

My mother was born in downtown Dallas, October 1, 1894. Her father owned and operated a bakery on Main Street across from the court house. The bakery was downstairs. The family was upstairs. That was the way people lived in those days. Babies were born at home, so my mother was born upstairs over a bakery. Being a true Southern lady, she would say, "Don't tell anyone I was born over a bakery. That's common." Woe be to anyone who was common. According to my mother, the worst thing anyone could possibly be was common. "Those people are common." "That's so common." I heard those expressions all of my life. Later on, my mother told everyone she was born over the bakery. It made her a Dallas pioneer. That was classy, and my mother was in constant pursuit of classiness!

2

Because Mother was born downtown and grew up downtown, she had great stories of early Dallas, and she told those stories over and over and over and over. The older she got, the more she told the stories. "Did I tell you this story?" "Yes, Mother, you've told that story." "Good, I'm going to tell it again. I want to hear it myself."

Guess what? I'm doing the same with my children today except, I'm more direct and I hit where it hurts. "Did I tell you this story?" "Yes, Mother, you've told that story." "Well, I'm going to tell it again, and if you don't listen, you're out of the will!" Suddenly, I have everyone's attention.

When my mother was a kid she often went to the Majestic Theatre on Elm Street to see vaudeville shows. One of the comedy skits she saw featured the usual, infamous baggy pants comedian. After a particular act, the funny man addressed the audience. "Gee, I hope you like my little get up!" My mother always remembered that phrase, and it became a family phrase. Everytime anyone of us did something creative, we'd always say, "Gee, I hope you like my little get up." Well, now, I bring you my story of Big D. It's not a comprehensive history of the city, although I must say, it borders on being one. It's an anecdotal history, and I'm including some of the stories I've told and some of the stories I've heard. There are many, many more. I just happened to bring these to mind and together. And as the comedian would say, "Gee, I hope you like my little get up!"

THE BAKER, THE MILLER, AND THE JAMES BROTHERS

My grandfather, William Hass, a baker by trade, came to Dallas in 1880. First, he worked for a friend who owned the Star Bakery on Elm Street. Grandpa worked hard, saved his money, and finally opened his own bakery on Main Street across from Old Red. He called it the West End Bakery. The building was torn down to build the Kennedy Memorial, but, alas, Grandpa sold the property many years before. Had he held on to it, I might have a bundle of money. But as the old adage states, "Money doesn't buy happiness." Ha! Ha! Ha!

Nevertheless, Grandpa prided himself in his fine bread, rolls, cakes and cookies. Later, there were other fine bakers who pros-

3

pered in Dallas — the Schepps and the Golmans to name two. But, Grandpa held his own with the competition.

The most important ingredient for bread naturally was flour, and most of the flour for the early Dallas bakers came from the Overton Mill. Aaron Overton came with his family to Dallas from Missouri in 1844. He operated the first flour mill in Dallas County using the water source at Kidd Springs. Business was good, because the records show that he milled 100 bushels of wheat a day. Overton's son, William Perry Overton, married Martha Ann Newton in 1847. They had seven children before she died. He then married a woman 30 years his junior. He wasn't taking any chances of being a widower again.

Both father and son took time off in 1850 to go to California as gold prospectors. Acquiring gold was the dream of many early Dallasites, including our founder, John Neely Bryan. Bryan went to California at least three times to claim a fortune. He returned each time penniless. The Overtons only tried once. They came back and decided that milling flour was a much more reliable way of making money.

During the outbreak of the Civil War in 1860, the Confederacy immediately recognized Dallas as a center of one of the important food-producing counties of Texas. A general quartermaster and commissary headquarters was established for the Army of the Trans-Mississippi. Overton Flour was vital for the war effort.

Dallas also became the center for organizing regiments of infantry, cavalry, and artillery composed of men from all over North Texas. In spite of the drain on manpower by the army, military activities kept the population up to prewar level during the early years of the war. These same activities actually increased the population of Dallas toward the end of the war. The original half a mile square of Bryan's town was extended to one and a half by two and a quarter miles. Rooms were needed all during the war for quarters. The Overton home was opened for the men.

After the war, Texas went into what I've always called the rootin', tootin' time — the time of cowboys and bandits. The James Brothers rode through Dallas. Infamous Jessie was impressed with Perry Overton, because the Dallas miller had an outstanding draw. He never missed his target!

Later, Frank James came through Dallas and stayed a while at the Overton house. Frank became ill and had to stay longer than he planned. After his recovery, he stayed even longer to work as a salesman at Sanger Brother, the dry goods store.

Alex Sanger was the first merchant in the South to adopt the rule of strictly one price — no bargaining! One Sanger customer remembered that in 1898 he heard a man bargaining with a clerk. The clerk suddenly shouted, "I'll wrap this suit up for $20 and not one cent less." The man shut up, took the suit, and paid the clerk — Frank James. From then on, prices were set!

The Overton children stayed in the Dallas area, and Grandson William dabbled in several different businesses — sugar and banking to name a couple.

GRANDPA ONLY SMOKED ON SUNDAYS

In 1612, John Rolfe, who married Pocahontas, planted and harvested the first truly successful tobacco crop in the colony of Virginia. This was the beginning of the tobacco industry and also the beginning of tobacco-related diseases. The American Cancer Society curses the day this crop came in. However, it was really several centuries before man and woman became addicted to the use of tobacco. Actually, only an occasional peace pipe was smoked or a pleasing "chaw" was taken. Smoking was done primarily at leisure and an early American really didn't have that much leisure to become addicted to anything except hard work. And work wasn't an addiction. It was a necessity.

Actually, heavy smoking became part of American culture during and after World War II. The movies were a big encouragement. If Humphrey Bogart could do it and look so manly, so could any other deserving male. If Joan Crawford could look sexy blowing smoke into the face of John Garfield, so could any American woman. Then the young people got involved, and Americans realized that they were hooked.

My grandfather smoked cigars but only on Sunday afternoons. He, like many other businessmen, put in a hundred hour week, so he really didn't have time to smoke. Ah! But on Sunday afternoon, he took off, sat down in the living room and smoked his cigar. There were some Sundays that he was deprived of his well earned stogie. If the preacher happened to come by, he could not light up. My mother remembered her mother calling from the front of the house, "Papa, quick, put out your cigar. The preacher is coming up

5

the walk!" His smoke was cut short. The cigar was out and the preacher was in. Better luck, next Sunday, Grandpa!

OLD RED

In 1992, Old Red, the Dallas County Courthouse, will be 100 years old. My mother oftèn bragged about the fact that she, as a child, learned to tell time from the clock on the top. "They ruined the building when they took the clock and the tower off," she complained. That clock meant a lot to my mother, so she was distressed over its removal in 1919. She really didn't care that the building was ready to collapse with the weight of the clock tower. She didn't even notice that the clock didn't run any longer. That tower was a part of her childhood and she wanted it there.

There was a rumor that the clock really stopped when a convicted man, Burl Oats, said it would stop if he were hanged. He continued to profess his innocence to the end. Well, he was hanged and the clock did stop. Factory men from St. Louis were sent to repair it, but by this time the tower was cracked and the clock's mechanism was uneven. The men decided that it could never run again, so it was best for the tower to be removed.

Mother saw a lot of action in front of that old courthouse. It was very exciting on Saturdays when all the farmers came into town and there were stray auctions held on or near the courthouse lawn. Mother saw Carrie Nation in 1904, go in for her lecture in one of the court rooms.

On the top of Old Red are decorations — gargoyles. Actually, they are not Gargoyles or Griffins as one may think. They are Wyverns. Gargoyles usually have water spouting from their lion-like mouths. Griffins are usually found guarding tombs or treasures. Besides, a Griffin has the head of an eagle. On top of the Dallas County Courthouse, one sees Wyverns. They are dragon-like with a human body curling into the tail. The Dallas Historical Society has made to sell small Wyvern statues that can be used as book ends, paper weights, or anything else one can do with a small Wyvern. I have one and I'm very fond of it. It just sits there on my desk and looks at me.

Maximilian A. Orlopp, Jr., designed and built the courthouse. He was orginally from Little Rock, but he later lived in Fort Worth. The whole structure was constructed in 1892 for $350,000.

THE ELLIS COUNTY COURTHOUSE

The Dallas County Courthouse has Wyverns on it. The one in Waxahachie, Ellis County, has faces — distorted faces. The people of Waxahachie are proud of those faces now. They furnish a great story. But when the citizenry first discovered them they weren't too happy. One of the stone carvers who was working on the Ellis County Courthouse, Harry Hurley, fell in love with a local girl, Mabel Frame. Her parents didn't want her mixed up with a roving stone cutter, so they would not allow Mabel to get near Harry. This angered Harry enough to carve faces into the courthouse — distorted faces of the very town folk that objected to him. No one knew about the faces until Harry was safely out of town. The town folk were enraged when they saw themselves with crossed eyes, sagging lips, warts on noses, etc. Now, today, the people of Waxahachie show off the faces, but a healing time had to transpire before they could accept this unsolicited art!

Besides this courthouse with the rare carvings, Waxahachie also has the last of the Chautauqua houses. In this auditorium William Jennings Bryan gave his notorious orations. Will Rogers spun a few yarns. All the performers on the circuit played Waxahachie. I just wonder if they learned to spell the name, Waxahachie, while they were there. There's an old joke. "What ever happened to the sheriff who finally learned to spell Waxahachie?" The answer — "He was moved to Nacogdoches!"

AUNT BINEY

My mother was very proud of the fact that she knew a freed slave. Her name was Aunt Biney and she worked for my grandfather as cook in the bakery. Mother shared many an hour with Aunt Biney who told mother all about plantation life in the South. Because Biney was tutored with the master's children, she could read and write. She was also very musical. The treat of the day came when Aunt Biney got out her guitar and sang for the family. On hot summer nights, she would sit right out on Main Street and strum and sing for the kids and for anyone else that wanted to stop and listen. My mother often pointed out, "Aunt Biney could really play her guitar and belt a song. Why, she was better than Glen Campbell!" Mother loved Glen Campbell's television show in the 60s. I guess when he would strum and sing, mother would remember Aunt Biney.

Aunt Biney had two sons who grew up to become professional chefs — one serving at the Adolphus Hotel and the other at the Oriental Hotel.

ENTERTAINMENT

When my mother was 13 years old, she found great delight in tattling on her 16 year old brother, Carl, who on occasion came sneaking out of the Happy Hour Theatre. This theatre was located on the northeast corner of Elm and Akard.

The Happy Hour was a house of burlesque. My uncle Carl and his buddies often treated themselves to the sight of some well endowed, yet skimpily-clad girls. Mother loved to rush home to tell her mother and father, fine upstanding Christian people, that Carl and the guys, who were also fine upstanding Christians, had gone to this den of iniquity. This was about the worst thing that bunch of guys ever did in Dallas in 1906.

The Happy Hour, with its burlesque queens, florished until the movie houses took over. People were way more interested in seeing pictures that moved than in seeing girls that stripped. Buster Keaton, Charlie Chaplin and Mary Pickford, because they moved on the screen, won out over burlesque.

At that same time in Dallas on up Elm Street, was the vaudeville house — the Majestic Theatre. The Majestic was the respectable house of entertainment. Here's where the singers, tap dancers, magicians, orators, and others with various acts held forth. These people all performed with their clothes on. This magnificent theatre, The Majestic, has been totally restored to its original grandeur and today Broadway shows are presented there for the citizens of Dallas.

A PUBLIC HANGING

In Dallas on May 12, 1905, Holly Van was executed — hanged. My mother, then a child of 12, was there. She witnessed the whole thing. It's hard to believe that only 80 years ago, there were public executions in America, but this one surely occurred.

Holly Van was a heavy drinker and one day he walked into Sol

Arnoff's store and killed him for the money in the cash drawer. In a couple of days, Van was caught, tried, and soon he was hanged in the county jail on Houston Street. Tickets for the execution were issued, and my mother got one. She was there when the floor dropped from under Holly Van and he was hanged by the neck until dead. There were so many people crammed into the jailhouse to see this that some almost suffocated. There was also a large crowd outside the jailhouse hoping to get a glimpse of something sensational.

Before his execution, Holly Van gave reasons for his wicked life. He said that drink and bad associates brought about his ruin. Father Hayes of Sacred Heart Cathedral heard Van's last confession and walked him to the scaffold.

The law officer that captured Van was Arthur Lee Ledbetter, Dallas County Sheriff from 1904–1910. Ledbetter was the second Dallas native to serve in that position. (The other was Lee Hinton Hughes who served from 1900–1901. Hughes succeeded Ben Cabell who resigned as Sheriff to become Mayor.)

Well, they say that seeing an execution is a deterrent of crime. That could be. I don't ever remember by mother committing murder.

AN 1898 FLASHER!

My mother's best friend when she was growing up was Lena Balisteri. The Balisteri family came to Dallas in 1880 from Italy, and Mr. Balisteri had a grocery store next to my grandfather's bakery on Main Street. When the two little girls, Lena and my mother, Amy, were not in school, they hung around the bakery or the grocery store. There was always something to do and see downtown.

One day, a lady came into the grocery store and began to dig brutally through the tomatoes. Mr. Balisteri, who spoke very little English, but who was a very polite and accommodating man, pleaded with the woman in a gentle way by saying, "Easy-mum — easy." The lady continued her digging until she finally asked mama what he was saying. "He wants you to go easy on the tomatoes. You're bruising the goods lady." The lady apologized and continued selecting the vegetables very tenderly.

One spring day, 1898, my mother and Lena were walking home from school. They attended the Colombian Elementary School on Akard Street where the convention center stands today. This is across from the cemetery where the first Dallasites are buried.

Actually, this site was pretty far out of town then. The city decided to put the dead and the kids out on Akard. Neveretheless, one day while walking home from school, Lena and mother met a flasher — an 1898 pervert. To be blunt, a guy exposed himself to the little girls. Well, they ran home to tell their fathers. When the baker and the grocer heard what had happened to their daughters, they didn't call the police. They got loaded shot guns off the wall and went down Akard Street in search of the depraved man. They fired off the guns several times. They didn't hit anyone, but you can rest assured that there were no flashers in the neighborhood for several years.

Law and order did exist in those days, but frequently people still took the law into their own hands, and nothing really was said about it.

Dallas had not yet turned from frontier ways, even though the chief of police, E. G. Cornwell, was working on it. Chief Cornwell gained his fame in law enforcement while he was working as a night watchman for the Texas Express Company. In 1892, a police officer, W. H. Riddell, was shot and killed by a Dallas shoemaker named Franklin Miller. The outcry in the city over the incident began to sound like the cry of a lynch mob. Miller barricaded himself in his shoe shop. The crowd outside was determined to hang him without a trial. E. G. Cornwell, the nightwatchman, was able to talk Miller into surrendering. Cornwell eventually became a police officer, then the assistant chief, then the constable of Precinct No. 1, and then Chief of the Dallas Police Force in 1898.

Oh, and by the way, to finish this whole story, my mother's friend, Lena Balisteri, grew up to marry a fine business man and real estate tycoon by the name of Desco. A street in North Dallas, Desco Drive, bears his name. I can't drive down that street without thinking of perverts, lynch mobs, and tomatoes.

LAKE CLIFF CASINO

In 1906, Charles A. Mangold, J. F. Zang, and several other well known citizens living in Oak Cliff acquired the area known as Lake Cliff. They turned the land into an amusement park which became very popular with the entire city. It was the Lake Cliff Casino. My mother and her friends frequented this entertainment hot spot.

There was a floating pool and bathhouse on the lake, and carnival rides encircled the whole plot. On Sunday afternoon, people gathered for balloon ascensions. Occasionally citizens were treated to an extrordinary sight. A daring soul would put on a parachute, rise in the balloon, jump, and float down to the cheering crowd.

There were band concerts, of course. The great March King, John Phillip Sousa, made band music extremely popular at the turn of the century. Families enjoyed picnicking on the rolling green lawn as they listened to the oom-pah-pahs.

At one time Lake Cliff had three theatres in operation. One featured light opera, another presented stock companies, and a third was for that new fangled thing called a motion picture. The third theatre was small because most people agreed that the motion picture was just a fad. It would eventually disappear.

My mother recalled seeing a very melodramatic presentation of *Carmen* at Lake Cliff in 1906. "When those house lights dimmed and the orchestra played the overture, I thought I was in paradise. We sat rigid in our seats — spellbound." That audience knew from the prelude music which switched from joyfulness to foreboding that something tragic was going to happen, and of course, it did. The feeling of impending doom hung over those theatre goers. On stage the fiery Carmen was the darling of the show. First, she flirted with José. Then in Act II she took up with Escamillo, the toreador. In Act III, José in a fit of jealousy stabbed the capricious beauty and then sobbed violently over her lifeless body. Dallas sobbed with him. Mother recalled a terrific moment when the dying Carmen sang, "I really loved you, José!" Alas, it was too late. The knife was in her. What a moment for Lake Cliff.

Meanwhile in the other theatre, my mother recalled the production of *Uncle Tom's Cabin*. A traveling stock company presented this play. On that stage Litle Eva fell through the ice and Uncle Tom saved her. This was another tense moment in dramatic history. It looked like Eva was a goner, but, alas, Uncle Tom in the nick of time came to the rescue. My mother spoke often of that production and she always mentioned that she was impressed with the ice. The sets and props of the day were very realistic. Whatever Eva fell through, it really looked like real ice. "I can still see that child waving her arms."

This theatre also posted listings of the famed Eastern Orpheum circuit of vaudeville. The greats played Dallas at Lake Cliff — greats like Al Jolson.

In the movie house the silent stars appeared — Charlie Chaplin, Buster Keaton, Fatty Arbuckle. "It was such fun to see Fatty Arbuckle flirt with a beauty, only to be dragged off by his battle ax wife at the end of the reel," Mother remembered.

BERNHARDT PLAYED DALLAS

Mother often announced, "I saw Sarah Bernhardt in a tent!" I remember that I shrugged that statement off with, "That can't be true." My mother went on bragging. "Oh, yes. It's true. There was a big tent at the Fair Park, and Bernhardt played in it. I remember it vividly. My aunt loved to go to plays, so she took me to see the great Bernhardt, and I'm telling you — Bernhardt was in a tent. Aunt Elsie took me!"

I never thought much about this. Actually, I figured my mother had gotten a childish dream mixed with reality. But when I read a biography of Bernhardt much later, I found that the great actress did play Dallas in a tent. And that tent was out at the Fair Park. How could this be?

It all happened in 1905, the year Madame Sarah planned a second trip to the United States — the Farewell American Tour. She had acquired some new producers, the Shubert Brothers, Sam Lee and Jake.

The Shubert Brothers were bucking the all powerful Theatrical Syndicate then. They got Sarah to sign on the dotted line where she promised to play only Shubert Theatres while she was in the United States. Guess what? Dallas, a city on her tour, didn't have a Shubert Theatre, so the announcement was made. "Madame Bernhardt will play Dallas in a tent."

My mother was right. She wasn't dreaming. She hadn't been confused. She was telling the truth. Sarah Bernhardt played Dallas in a tent. The tent was out at the Fair Park, and my mother was in the audience.

When Sarah heard that she was going on in a tent, this didn't bother her in the least. She said that it was a genuine "Yankee" adventure. Europeans refer to all Americans as Yankees!

The tent seated over four thousand spectators. The stage was made in movable sections, the seats folded up, and the dressing rooms were like canvas bath houses. It was like a circus, and the Madame loved it. Railroad tracks were nearby, so the train simply pulled up with patrons from all over the state. They alit from the train and marched into the "Bernhardt Tent" for the show.

It wasn't easy acting. Sometimes rain pelted down on the white-top with the noise of a million snare drums, but this didn't stop Sarah. A Texas Norther blew in and unloosed the tent flaps. Still the show went on. A rootin', tootin' drunk cowboy once came in hollering, "I'm gonna see this Bernhardt gal an' her song-and-dance. It better be good." In spite of all these happenings, the troupe survived and made money.

Madam Sarah was a real trouper. I'm glad she came and survived the experience. After all, it gave my mother the chance to see the great Bernhardt perform in a tent in Dallas.

THE HOUSE ON WEST 10TH

At the height of my grandfather's business career, he was able to buy a home on West 10th. This was truly a classy area. In fact, mother always bragged about that house and the fine neighborhood in which it was located. "Why, we lived across the street from Judge Muse!" she'd boast. Judge E. B. Muse, an extremely controlled and proper person, was Judge of the 44th District Court. One newspaper stated that "he attained dignity and fame as he performed his duties." My mother claimed he attained dignity and fame when he moved on West 10th!

Judge Muse was a native of South Carolina. His father was a physician and a dentist of French Hugenot descent. The family moved to Texas, and Dr. Muse enjoyed the distinction of being the pioneer dentist of the State of Texas. Son, E. B., graduated from Baylor University in 1879. He read for the law and practiced that law first in Washington County before he came to Dallas.

The Muse house stands at 505 West 10th today completely restored. Father Lee at Christ Episcopal Church, which is across the street from the house, held the funeral services for Willard Muse, the last Muse to live in the house. My mother's house is gone. In fact, it burned. It's not there, but I have a feeling my mother in heaven is telling the heavenly hosts all about her house on West 10th.

13

MOTHER'S TELEVISION CAREER

When my mother was 84 years old, she started her career in television. Until then, she had just been a housewife. It all started when my agent, Joy Wyse, called me. A certain advertising agency was searching for odd looking people. "Get down there. You fit the bill." I had taken my mother to the grocery store that morning. The audition was at noon, so I didn't have time to take her home. Obviously, I was going to have to take her to the audition. She was thrilled to go. I sat her down and approached the throne of the casting agent. "I'm sure that I'm just what you want," I said to the stone faced judge of talent. His steel eyes pierced through me and fell upon my mother. "Who is this?" He asked. "Oh, that's my mother. I take her everywhere with me. She's just here."

"You ever make a commercial," he asked Mother. "Heavens, no," she laughingly responded. "Would you like to make one?" he seriously asked. The rest is history. Mother got the part. For four years she licked a Dairy Queen. It was a national commercial, so the money was terrific. Eventually, she got residual checks too. She was always amazed over the whole thing. "Just think. I got paid for all that fun."

After the Dairy Queen there were others. Southwest Airlines called and asked me if she could run after a jet. "Of course, she's only 85." Later there was a What-A-Burger commercial. At 88, she retired. "Let someone else do it," she sighed.

Mother lived 90 years, and she lived all of those years with great expectancy. She always felt that something exciting was just around the corner, and for her it always was.

CHAPTER II

Some of My Stories

A PIANO, A FLOOD, A HOTEL,
AND MARY GARDEN

Mornings were always very busy at my house when I was growing up. Mother fixed a great breakfast, Daddy left for the office quite early, and I practiced the piano. In order to get my "hour" in I would get up early and practice from six to seven. With all this activity, my father felt that he didn't have time to read the *Dallas Morning News,* so he only took the *Dallas Times Herald,* the evening paper. Daddy started taking the *News* because of a great selling pitch.

In those days, when I was practicing the piano, there was no air conditioning, so we opened the windows and doors. In the spring with warm weather arriving, the front door was always opened for ventilation, so my piano music floated out on the morning air, breaking the silence of the dawn. One day, the *Dallas Morning News* boy knocked on the door. My father, who didn't want me to lose one moment of precious practice time, rushed to answer. Daddy was greeted by a smiling face and an urgent voice. "Don't you want something to read while you're listening to that?" My father was so

15

impressed with the kid's selling pitch, he immediately subscribed to the *News* and read it faithfully even after I had left home and the piano practice had ended.

The piano upon which I practiced was a sturdy, old upright, solid mahogany, that was given to my mother by her anxious father when she was nine years old. It came from Bush & Gerts Piano Company on Christmas Eve, 1903. Mother immediately started taking piano lessons and like most kids eventually learned and remembered one piece, "Glow Worm." She played that number until she died. It was her piece. Everyone who has ever taken piano and who has not graced the concert stage, always knows one piece. Mine is "The Saber Dance." Mother called it the $5,000 piece, because it took that much money for me to learn it. Don't misunderstand. I had marvelous teachers. I just didn't turn out to be a concert pianist. However, to this day, I can entertain myself at home. That was something everyone wanted to be able to do. Remember those ads for quick piano success. "They laughed when I sat down to play." I can assure you, everyone to this day laughs when I sit down to play. Again, I want it understood that it was not my teachers. They were wonderful — Ludie Rae Gardner, Bertha Mendenhall (very well known Dallas name), and Ida Mae Hartman — in that order. Parents often switched teachers. They felt that the kid would be stimulated by someone new. Like most kids, I didn't need to be stimulated. I needed to practice! Changing teachers was an easy out!

Mother's piano on which I practiced went through the Dallas flood of 1908. She loved to tell of my grandfather frantically calling in the neighbors to help him put the piano on boxes, so it would not be ruined by the rushing, flood waters. Dallas completely went under water in 1908. When the waters receded, the city started building the levees. When the levees were completed the Trinity River was under control as far as downtown was concerned. There are still areas in Dallas that experience flood waters. Hopefully, this situation will be corrected in the future. In the meantime, if you hear of anyone needing "The Saber Dance" played, call me! I still know it, and I perform free of charge even though my father invested $5,000 in piano lessons. And, by the way, I still have my mother's piano.

While we're on the subject of music, piano, and downtown Dallas, I feel that it's appropriate to mention a grand recital and social event that happened in 1911. The gorgeous Adolphus Hotel opened. It was built by Adolphus Busch, of the famous brewing family of Anheuser-Busch. The hotel was spectacular. It was magnificent then and it still is. High tea is served every afternoon, and I can assure you that the Adolphus Lobby is an elegant spot to sip tea. My mother was at the first high tea served in the Adolphus, Spring, 1911. The hotel opened with the glorious opera star, Mary Garden, singing in the lobby while the elite of Dallas listened and sipped the fine brew. Miss Garden was a Scottish-born soprano of the finest quality. She was noted for her dramatic vocal ability. In fact, she won the part of Melisande in the Debussy opera *Pelleas et Melisande*. Maureice Maeterlinck, the master playwright wrote the play and Debussy put it to music in 1902. Maeterlinck insisted that his mistress sing the Melisande role, but Debussy demanded that Mary Garden portray the character. Miss Garden won the role and Maeterlinck and Debussy never spoke to each other again.

This charmer and very talented singer, Mary Garden, in 1911, entertained the crowds at the Adolphus! Fortunately, my mother was there.

Much later, in 1951, I was privileged to see Miss Garden when she came to the University of North Texas to assist in the direction of the opera, *The Daughter of the Regiment*. Mary McCormic, director of the opera workshop at the university, was a protegee of Miss Garden's. My husband, who then was just a favorite boy friend, was the timpanist in the orchestra that accompanied the opera. It was a marvelous evening for all, and fortunately, we were there!

A TWO BIT SANTA

Christmas, 1932, was a bleak one. Unemployment reached between 15 and 17 million by the year's end. Thirty-four million Americans had no income of any kind, and Americans who did work averaged little more than $16 per week, down from $28 a week in 1929. Breadlines formed in many cities. Some 1,616 banks failed. For relief, Congress passed the Home Loan Act, which established 12 Federal Home Loan Banks that would lend money to mortgage loan institutions. This measure was designed to rescue the banks that were being forced to close.

Nearly 20,000 business firms went bankrupt, and the expenditures for food and tobacco fell 10 billion dollars below the 1929 total, and the U.S. Gross National Product fell to 41 billion, just over half the 1929 level. The Dow Jones dropped to the lowest point it would reach during this Great Depression.

The U.S. motor car sales fell to just one million, down from five million in 1929. Ford and General Motors laid off thousands of workers. My daddy was working for McColister Chevrolet, 901 S. Ervay, and that Christmas the car sales were really down. In fact, Daddy had one quarter in his pocket. Late in the afternoon, Christmas eve, a man came into the show room with a Santa Claus statue about three feet tall made of chalk. Brightly painted chalk sculptures were very popular then. The man was desperate to sell that Santa. Daddy asked him how much he wanted for the work of art. "Two bits — one quarter!" It was all my daddy had in his pocket, but he bought it for me. Of course, I still have that Santa Claus, and it's in mint condition. It stands all year long, not just at Christmas time, at the fireplace in my house. Antique dealers consider it quite valuable. It's worth a million dollars to me. Times were bleak in 1932, but not so bleak that my daddy wouldn't spend his last quarter for a Santa Claus for me!

THE MEANING OF LIFE

My mother gave me the meaning of life in one sentence. She received this valued counsel from one of her father's customers. Mother was about ten years old and was helping out in the bakery. A man came in. My grandfather immediately recognized him and greeted him with a hearty, "Hi, how are you doing?" The man proceeded to tell my grandfather just how he was doing. "How am I doing? I'll tell you how I'm doing. I'm in terrible condition. You know what life is? It's one *damn* thing after another."

My mother's ears perked up at once. She had never cussed. No one in the family had ever cussed. Four letter words were not allowed in their household, but here was this man. He dared to come in and cuss. He described life as being one *damn* thing after another.

My mother never forgot that man. In fact, she was truly grateful that he had shared his insight into the human condition with her and her daddy. "I'm glad that man came in that day, because, you

18

see, my dear, that man was right. You know what life is — one *damn* thing after another."

I'm truly thankful that my mother shared this story with me, because I too have discovered that when I solve one problem there is always another one waiting for me. St. Paul said it so well in Romans 5:4. "Suffering produces endurance, and endurance produces character, and character produces hope."

THE MEANING OF LIFE, PART 2

My mother told me, "There are two things that will make you secure on this earth. Have faith in God and get your teacher's certificate." Well, I went to Sunday School and church and found the Lord. Then I went to college and got my *permanent* teacher's certificate, 1952. Unfortunately, today, that certificate is not valid. The whole educational system has changed drastically. The whole world has changed drastically. There is no such thing as a *permanent* teacher's certificate. Educators, as well as other professionals, must go back to school, take refresher courses, must take tests to qualify for various positions. Nothing is *permanent* today. It's all *change, change, change.* We all must endure it. This sudden and rapid change in today's world is something we all must learn to expect. It has caused the disease of the 80s — *stress!* And guess what? There's more coming — more *stress.*

Well, the new systems have taken away my teacher's certificate. All I've got left is God!

NATURAL SPAS!

I grew up with Mary Heffington Godfrey who had a very nice aunt named Johnnie. I remember that Aunt Johnnie was constantly going to Glen Rose, Texas, to bathe, and Mary got to go with her. How I envied Mary her trips to Glen Rose, for you see, my family didn't bathe — at least not in the mineral waters that flowed so freely in Somervell County. I asked my mother why we didn't go to Glen Rose to bathe, and she said, "We don't need it," and that was that. Evidently, my family could do without dips into those healing springs.

Early explorers found the land in and around Glen Rose heavily populated with Indians. Those Indians knew a good thing when they had it — healing waters. There's a creek in that county, Squaw Creek, named for the Indian women who resided around this natural health club.

My piano teacher was also a bather. She went down to Marlin, Texas, for her healing soaks. Again, I envied her the trips. Explorers found lots of agile Indians around what was to become Falls County. It was the artesian water there that gave those Indians their vim and vigor. Those waters certainly did wonders for my piano teacher. After her Marlin trips she was always able to battle all those kids that constantly played sour notes.

My mother had friends who were always going up to Hot Springs, Arkansas, for baths. There were lots of these God-given spas around, but the grandaddy of all spas was in Mineral Wells, Texas. This little town, 35 miles west of Fort Worth offered Crazy Water Crystals.

The crazy story started on Christmas eve in 1877 when Judge J. A. Lynch brought his family to Palo Pinto County in a covered wagon. He arrived not far from the home of Oliver Loving, who with Charles Goodnight was the first trail driver of Texas cattle. For a long time the Lynch family had to haul their water from the Brazos River, almost four miles away from their house. Judge Lynch finally dug a well, but he was afraid to drink the water. It had an odd taste. However, Mrs. Lynch was so tired of hauling water, she went on and drank the water from the well. Soon she found that her rheumatism had completely disappeared. Could it be the water? Other pioneers came to test the healing powers of this water. One woman who was just a tad "off" seemed to regain her mental powers as she continued to drink from the mineral fountain. Folks around began to call the well the Crazy Woman Well, later cutting the name to Crazy Well. The Lynch family wanting to get rid of the "crazy" aspect, called the town that grew up around the well, Mineral Wells.

The town continued to grow with the story of the crazy woman. Boarding houses sprang up everywhere to accommodate the travelers who were seeking this liquid cure-all. In 1912, a grand hotel was built called the Crazy Hotel. All the guests were given the water from the original well. More accommodations were added until the town boasted more hotels than homes. The word Crazy took over — Crazy Theatre, Crazy Well Drinking Pavilion, Crazy Well Bath House, Crazy Well State Bank, Crazy Laundry and Cleaning — everything was Crazy.

The health business boomed in Mineral Wells all through the early 20s, but in 1925, the hotel burned to the ground. One Texan, very upset over this loss, was the wealthy Dallas insurance man, Carr P. Collins. He was sorry that the hotel burned, but he saw a good business opportunity. He bought the charred real estate and soon erected a hotel more magnificent than the original.

The slogan, "Come to the Crazy Hotel and drink your way to health," was painted on a banner that waved over the new hotel when it opened in 1927. It was a seven-story building with 200 rooms, a huge lobby, a ballroom, a roof garden for dancing, a mineral bath department, and the Crazy Water Bar, where a guest could drink the powerful liquid. Celebrities came to Mineral Wells — Judy Garland, Tom Mix, Jean Harlowe, Marlene Dietrich, General John J. Pershing, Will Rogers, and D. W. Griffith. Finally, the water was crystallized and sold everywhere.

Hal Collins, Carr P.'s brother, was in charge of advertising. He sponsored a country music show on the radio, and he went on the air himself with this pitch. "When I was a kid, I had a shotgun, and when that shotgun got clogged up, I'd give it a good cleaning. This is what Crazy Water does for your body   it cleans it when it's clogged up."

The professional advertising men were horrified. "That ad is too home spun. It's crude and should be off the air." But when Hal did go off and no longer mentioned his clogged gun and body, the switchboard at the station lighted up. The public missed the gun story. That ad was the best part of the show.

Well, today people have their own built in spas, jacuzzis! The hotel in Mineral Wells is boarded up with a barbed wire fence around it. NO BATHS!

A FRIEND, A MOVIE, AND A SOAPBOX

My good buddy, Charles Roffino, and I grew up in the Arcadia Theatre on Greenville Avenue. We went to the movies every Saturday afternoon first and foremost to experience airconditioning. Then we went to see our other friends. Then we went for the movie, the serial, the cartoon, and the advertisements. Because there was no television, the ads in the movies were the only video commercials we ever saw. Just like kids today who watch television ads, we had the ads memorized. Kids today, of course, have so many more to watch and commit to memory. We had only a few. Our favorite ad on Saturday at the movie was the White Star Laundry commercial. It showed first, the pick up and delivery man, second, the housewife gladly giving her clothes to this man, and third, the inside of the spotless laundry. Then came the climax. A little kid pointed to the White Star Laundry and said, "That's my mama's laundry." We waited for that child to come on. Then in a grand, speaking choir, every kid in the Arcadia would say along with the kid on the screen, "That's my mama's laundry." What a moment! We did the same thing every Saturday and loved it. I remember the only change that came was when the movie, *The Mummy's Curse,* was showing. Then when the laundry kid came on, we said all together, "That's my *mummy's* laundry." This was even a bigger moment! Finally, when we had forgotten about *The Mummy's Curse,* we went back to the proper and original statement.

Charles Roffino, my neighbor, friend, and movie companion, with his brother, Tony Roffino, grew up to build many, many, many houses in East Dallas. Charles was always a true genius when it came to building things. A whiz kid with cartons. He could make cars, doll furniture, anything out of boxes, crates, or anything else that was thrown out. One summer he made the neatest soapbox car that anyone had ever seen. He should have entered it in the derby, because he would have won hands down.

It just so happened that Mrs. Roffino that summer decided to redo her bathroom. The contractor tore out the old beaver board walls that were made to look like genuine tile. The color, of course, was that sick, pea green that was so popular in bathrooms at that time. Depression green — I believe it was called. No one has ever used that color since. Nevertheless, Charles took those discarded boards and made a car. The wheels came from our old beat up tricycles. It was a rare sight when Charles Roffino coasted down the street in a tile car! You'd never see that today.

LINDA DARNELL

I have an autographed picture of Linda Darnell. How about that? For all you youngsters in the reading audience, Linda Darnell was a beautiful Dallas girl who was whisked off to Hollywood in 1940. Many people have asked, "How did you get an autographed picture of Linda Darnell?" Well, it wasn't easy.

During the first part of the 20th century, besides measles and chickenpox, children *took* expression lessons. (Before this time, the lessons were termed "elocution" instructions.) I remember the day I started my class. Mother turned to me and said, "Rose-Mary, we're going to bring you out!" It sounded rather ominous, but since I trusted my mother and felt that I had nothing to lose, I went on with her to the Woodrow School of Expression and Dramatic Arts. Mrs. O. D. Woodrow, teacher, welcomed a whole mob of kids who obviously with me also needed "bringing out." She gave us copies of poems and short essays which we glued into our new expression notebooks. She called these poems and essays "readings" or "little pieces." We were to memorize these pieces and at our next lesson we were to recite them in clear, rounded tones using appropriate gestures. How far one was "brought out" depended entirely on how clear the tones were and how appropriate the gestures could be.

Well, it just so happened that Linda Darnell was in that class. She gave readings with us. In fact, she was so "brought out," she was swept off to Hollywood. Me? I'm still giving readings and pieces. *But I'm alive!* Poor Linda, She lived on the fast track and then died very tragically.

Nevertheless, Linda gave a sensational performance as Amber in the movie adaptation of the sizzling best seller, *Forever Amber.* Then she returned to Dallas to meet and greet her friends and to promote the movie. Somehow, Mrs. Woodrow wrangled an audience with the star and invited the old expression gang to go down with her to the Adolphus Hotel to see Linda. Mrs. Woodrow composed a cheer for us to give as Linda stepped off the elevator into the hotel lobby. The class met together two hours before Linda was to see us, so that we could learn the cheer.

Can you imagine a mob of kids learning a cheer in the lobby of the Adolphus? In those days, children never spoke their minds. We kids thought the whole thing was dumb, but we never told Mrs. Woodrow. We just learned the cheer. It was to be given in clear rounded tones with all the appropriate gestures. Arms and hands waved violently to the left as we shouted, "Dallas's Linda!" Arms and hands waved violently to the right as we shouted, "Texas's Linda!" Arms and hands waved violently upward as we shouted, "Our Linda!" We had it down perfectly.

Finally, it was time for Linda to descend from the penthouse

23

suite. Elevators, in those days, had hands like a clock that told exactly on what floor the elevator was situated. The hand pointed to the penthouse. Linda was getting on. It swept downward. She was on the first floor. The door opened and she stepped out. We gave the cheer. Linda went into shock and started signing 8 x 10 glossies, and that's how I got my autographed picture of Linda Darnell. My good friend, Peggy Branan Cox, was in this class and she claims she doesn't remember any of this. I assured her that she was there. She has just blotted it out of her mind. Can you blame her?

THE DAY OF INFAMY

At the turn of the century, many Japanese came to our country to escape the misery brought on by the wars that raged in the eastern part of the world. In 1900 Mr. and Mrs. Hideo Muta came to Texas from Japan and opened the Oriental Art Company at 1312 Elm Street, Dallas, Texas. They imported and sold beautiful articles from their homeland. My mother knew the Mutas well. She grew up with their children.

In 1925, the Oriental Art Shop had an anniversary party. Everyone who came into the store was given a lovely blue vase with a white dove on the side. My mother was there and she got the vase which I now possess. On the bottom of the vase there is stamped, "Oriental Art Shop, 25th Anniversary," with another familiar phrase of the time, "Made in Japan."

For Christmas, 1941, I decided that I wanted a Japanese doll. Mother went down to the Oriental Art Shop on December 1 to buy the doll. In those days people put things on layaway, so Mother paid half the price for the doll and agreed to pay the rest on December 23, when she picked up the merchandise.

On December 7, Pearl Harbor was bombed by the Japanese. On December 8, the Oriental Art Shop, which had been in existence since 1900, was closed and the Mutas were held by the U.S. Government. They with the other 120,000 Japanese Americans in the country were hustled off to camps that offered very primitive quarters to people who had prospered as American citizens and who had been living very well.

Now, I am aware that on December 7th, hundreds of American lives were snuffed out without warning, but still these Japanese people who had come at the turn of the century to our country had nothing to do with the war. I am also aware that American POWs suffered greatly in Japanese prison camps. These men surely could never forget their days of torture. Still, these Japanese Americans had nothing to do with that situation. There were all sorts of rumors that sprang up after the bombing. Japanese gardeners in California supposedly planted arrow shaped patches that pointed the way to defense plants. These arrows could be seen from the air. There was also a rumor that the Japanese were learning German so they could help the Nazis. Of course, there was no truth in any of these accusations.

Mother went down on the 23rd of December, and the doll was given to her by a government officer. I never played with the doll, since a Japanese doll wasn't a popular item after December 7, 1941. It's in my doll collection today in mint condition.

Mother never knew what happened to the Mutas. There are only 60,000 of these Japanese Americans alive today. In 1988, President Reagan signed H.R. 442. This rule was an apology to the Japanese Americans who were held captive here during the war. It granted $20,000 to each of them.

NOVEMBER 22, 1963

What were you doing that November day in 1963 when the President of the United States was shot? I was teaching at Bishop Dunne High School. A student rushed into my classroom with the news of the tragedy. Bishop Dunne was a Catholic High School, so the priests immediately performed all the religious rites that were proper for such a catastrophe. Prayers were said by everyone, and then school was dismissed. My children, who were eight and nine years of age, came home from their school, and I met them in the front yard. I remember my neighbor just down the street, police officer J. D. Tippit, was backing out of his driveway in his squad car. I waved. Officer Tippit had been ordered to the central area of Oak Cliff. Just one hour later he encountered Lee Harvey Oswald and was shot to death. The nation mourned the death of a president and also the death of an innocent police officer who just happened to stop the president's assassin. The nation opened its heart to Mrs. Marie Tippit and her children and sent them $650,000 in unsolicited contributions.

After shooting officer Tippit, Oswald dashed down Jefferson Blvd. and darted into the Texas Theatre. There he was apprehended by the Dallas Police.

My mother on that day had been on the corner of Main and Lamar in the large crowd waving to the President as he passed. My daddy was in his office window in the Mercantile Bank Building also waving to the President. Daddy got the news of the shooting first, and he called mother. She couldn't believe it. "But I just saw him an hour ago."

We all have our stories as to what we were doing on that fateful day in Dallas.

LAUREL LAND SUNRISE EASTER PAGEANT

One of the sweetest and dearest men in the whole wide world was Mr. Earl Widner, founder and owner of Laurel Land Cemetery. He was on the Board of Trustees at Dallas Baptist University when I was teaching there. The kids loved him because he drove a hearse that was almost bigger than he was. And too, he always wore a "shovel" tie clasp denoting his occupation — grave digger.

Well, nevertheless, in the spring of 1967, Mr. Widner came to Dr. Charles Pitts, president of Dallas Baptist University, with the sad news that the Laurel Land Sunrise Easter Pageant was not going to be presented any more.

This pageant had been held at Laurel Land on Easter morning since the 1930s. Mrs. Pearl Wallace Chappell, a drama teacher in Dallas, had written the pageant for her students and had convinced Mr. Widner that Laurel Land would be the perfect setting for the drama. After all, her students needed somewhere to perform and what better place than a cemetery!

Mr. Widner agreed to sponsor the pageant and eventually 10,000 people attended each year. For these people, it was part of their Easter celebration to bundle up — it was always cold at 3 AM on Easter morning — and come to Laurel Land for these very moving and spiritual presentations.

Now, after all these years, it looked like the pageant was not to be given any more. Mrs. Chappell was not well enough to direct the drama. The cast had grown with the audience, and it was physically hard to move a mob of people around on a mammoth stage and she just couldn't do it.

26

Mr. Widner was very distressed about the situation because he loved his pageant. After all, he built a permanent stage for this drama. Somehow there must be a way of keeping this fine tradition going. Maybe Charles Pitts had the answer.

Mr. Widner announced to Charles Pitts that he would give a large sum of money to the University provided the pageant would continue to be presented. Well now, we all know that every school needs money, so Dr. Pitts thanked Mr. Widner for his money and assured him that the show would go on.

"Get Rose-Mary in here," Dr. Pitts demanded of his secretary. In a moment, I was on the spot. "You will direct the Laurel Land Easter Pageant," Dr. Pitts simply stated. "I will?" I gasped.

Mr. Widner chimed into the conversation. "It's easy. You have only to gather 250 people together for three quick rehearsals, and on Easter morning at 3 AM, they all gather for makeup and costuming. Then they give the pageant."

Would you believe that I pulled it together that year and continued to pull it together for the next nine years?

After I got the assignment, I immediately went to Mrs. Chappell for help. She told me the names of people who had been in the pageant for over thirty years. They felt like they had been born into those roles. I definitely needed these people, because they knew more about the whole thing than I did. I called a lady who had been the angel since the beginning. She readily agreed to once again do the part. She finished our telephone conversation with this statement, "Of course, I'll be there, dear. I've always been the angel, and remember — I have my own wings."

For the mob I went to my classes at the college. "Do you all want to pass this course? Then, be in a robe on Easter morning at 3 AM at Laurel Land Cemetery. For extra credit, bring your mothers and fathers."

Somehow, I managed to create the attitude on the DBU campus that it was an honor to be in the pageant. A student rushed up to me and breathlessly asked, "How do you get into the Easter Pageant?" Another student standing nearby responded, "It's not how you get in — it's how you get out!"

If ever anyone appeared in the pageant, I would make certain, by hook or crook, they would come back each year. With only three rehearsals, I needed people who were familiar with all the ins and outs — especially the ins.

27

It was always muddy on Easter morning. It was muddy even if it didn't rain. The cast wore tennis shoes until they went on stage, and then they would change into sandals. One Easter, Pontius Pilate forgot to make the change. One student pointed this out to me. "Look, Mrs. Rumbley. There's Pilate in his U.S. Keds."

One Easter, the sound tape of the rooster crowing broke. There must be a rooster crowing after Peter's third denial. Well, I had to go on live with a crow. I wasn't very good. However, the next year, the sound man came with a new tape. He was so excited over it. He had gone out to a farm and had recorded a real rooster. It would have been perfect had he played it at the right speed. A rooster with a drawl isn't the greatest sound in the world.

When Restland bought out Laurel Land, the pageant came to an end for sure. The stage was going to be used for grave sites. I have often wondered if, when digging graves, those diggers didn't run into an old sandal or two that was lost in the mud those glorious years when I directed the Laurel Land Sunrise Easter Pageant.

DALLAS/HOLLYWOOD/BROADWAY

The minute I enrolled in that first expression and elocution class, I knew I wanted to be a star on the Broadway stage or the Hollywood screen. Well, instead of going to Hollywood/Broadway, I got married, had two kids, and taught school. But, before you start feeling sorry for me, I need to tell you about the changes that occurred in Dallas. In the first place, Broadway/ Hollywood came to me. Just when I decided to look for stardom — my kids were in school — the dinner theatres opened. I'm a fairly good character actress, so I played a couple of dinner theatres. Some of those people with whom I performed in the dinner theatres are now on Broadway. I'm not there, but I do know some great actors and actresses that are. Then, Mr. Tom Hughes called and I found myself with the stars of the Dallas Summer Musicals. And then, Mr. Peter Bogdanovich arrived on the scene.

Mr. Bogdanovich won all sort of acclaim in 1971 for his movie, *The Last Picture Show*. It was all filmed in Archer City, Texas. Because Bogdanovich did so well in Texas with that movie, he decided to come back in 1973 and cast a real classic, *Paper Moon*, starring Ryan O'Neal and his little daughter, Tatum. My

28

agent, Joy Wyse, called and told me that they were looking for some down home type women with thick Texas accents. That's me! I went to the audition and got the part of Tatum's aunt. Rent the film and you'll see me in the last scene of that movie. I open the door for little Tatum. In a heavy Texas accent I ask her if she wants a piece of pie. I also ask her if she wants to stay with me. She looks the place over and quickly runs back to Ryan O'Neal. Then the film ends. Tatum won an Academy Award for her role.

I was teaching theatre at Dallas Baptist University when *Paper Moon* was premiering in New York. I pointed this out to my class and then in jest said, "You ought to take up a collection and send me to New York for the premier." They did! Those kids took me seriously for the first time in my teaching career, took up a collection, and sent me to New York. I went to see *Paper Moon* with Ryan and Tatum O'Neal. Needless to say, it was a great moment in my life. I stepped off the plane in New York and a reporter was there. "Are you this school teacher from Texas that these kids have sent up here to see the movie." I responded, "Yep, that's me!" Off I went for a glorious and grand time in the Big Apple.

So you see, I have acted with Broadway stars, tap danced with Ginger Rogers, and appeared on screen with an Academy Award winning actress, and I've done all this in Dallas, Texas.

IRONY NEXT DOOR!

Dianne Carlson, an attorney for American Airlines, lives next door to me. This lady lawyer lives in a house once owned by Senator Claud C. Westerfeld. It just so happens that State Senator Westerfeld objected to the fact that in 1937 a woman held a judgeship on the Texas bench. That woman, of course, was Sarah T. Hughes. Judge Hughes as a child was told by her mother, "You can do anything you want to do." Sarah set out to do just that. This lady lawyer, Sarah, had her first successful political race in Dallas, 1930. She went everywhere campaigning with a $300 expense account. She won the election. During her third term in the house, Governor James Allred appointed Sarah to the Fourteenth District Court. She was an extremely effective judge, but this didn't make a difference with Senator Westerfeld even though Sarah went on to serve the State of Texas many years.

In 1961, Sarah T. was appointed to a federal judgeship — first female federal judge in the state. Westerfeld must have turned in his grave.

Then, on November 22, 1963, Judge Hughes administered the oath of office to her longtime friend, Lyndon B. Johnson. She may not have considered this her biggest moment, but the world certainly did. This was the first time a woman administered the oath of office to an American President. Claude Westerfeld turned again in his grave.

This man, Westerfeld, was obviously a chauvinist. Isn't it ironic that a lady lawyer lives in his old house?

IRONY IN THE NEIGHBORHOOD

My graduation class from North Dallas High School, 1949, had a 40th reunion in 1989. We had never had one before. We should not have waited so long, because when we got together, we had a terrific time. North Dallas High was named North Dallas because it was so far North of the city — way out on Cole, Haskell, and McKinney. The one thing that we all remembered was the building of North Central Expressway. This was such a big deal for the city. If we had a class on the third floor of the east side of the building, then we could watch the cranes, the giant diggers, the whole operation in action. Isn't it ironic that 40 years later, we're watching the whole thing dug up so that the old expressway can be widened. If you've ever wondered why the three lanes stop at Mockingbird, the answer is simple. The city stopped at Mockingbird. Why would they build an expressway any farther out? Later it was extended to accommodate a little traffic that went on farther Northward!!!! Two lanes were all that were needed.

SOUTH FORK

In 1984, when the TV series, Dallas, was at its peak, the Republican Party held its convention in our city to nominate once again Mr. Reagan for the presidency. That summer, the temperature climbed to 104 degrees. Protesters demanded a place and a time to protest. Dallas gave them the place and the time. They protested, had heat strokes, and left. We were glad. Dallas is always worried when a president comes to town. Nothing must happen to him.

30

Well, nevertheless, that summer, a tour agency called me and asked me to take the wives of Mr. Reagan's cabinet out to South Fork. I couldn't imagine why a group of intelligent, classy ladies would want to go out to J. R.'s spread, but I was willing to escort them out to the ranch. Personally, I always thought that you had to be out of your mind to go out to South Fork. If you had been out there and you were *not* out of your mind, then you only went because some relative or friend who was out of his mind came to town and wanted to go out there. Then you went.

Well, nevertheless, I took these ladies out there in 104 degree heat. We were on an air conditioned bus, of course. When we arrived, one lady decided that because her feet were hurting, she'd leave on her jellies. In 1984, plastic jellies (shoes) were all the rage. When that lady stepped off the bus in those jellies, she melted to J. R.'s asphalt. We had to chisel her out of J. R.'s driveway. After we freed her from the asphalt, she had the nerve to ask where Bobby and Pam were. Oh, well, I must admit that our city did get a lot of publicity from that show.

THAT AWFUL TEXAS ACCENT

A Texan can go anywhere in the world, open his mouth and speak, and anyone within earshot will exclaim, "Oh, you're from Texas." The accent is that distinguishing. When I went to college, the University of North Texas, my speech teacher, Myrtle Hardy, pleaded with all of us who were entering the field of communication, "Please rid yourselves of that uncultured Texas accent." Our reply was usually the same, "Now, *Miz* Hardy, that's *shore* hard to do!" We Texans do not have a Southern accent, we have a Texas accent. Those from the deep South — Tennessee, Alabama, Georgia, Mississippi — have a drawl, but they also speak with a soft *R*. Texans have a hard *R*, and this, with *iny* instead of *any* and *thang* instead of *thing*, makes for this very distinctive accent. Just why did this accent develop? Linguistic scholars have studied the situation and have come up with these conclusions. Primarily, three sets of people populated Texas. The Spanish came in 1520. When Stephen F. Austin made the deal with the Mexican government to colonize Texas in 1820, hundreds of people poured in from the South and from Germany. Remember, the German people had nothing in Europe at that time, so Texas seemed like a good deal to them. It was!

31

The families from the South were descended from the English settlers. That Southern drawl developed as these people drew farther and farther from their English roots. In other words, the drawl developed as a distortion of the English spoken in Europe. That's why English actresses can always play Southern ladies. They can hear that accent. Vivian Leigh, fine English lady, played Scarlette O'-Hara, fine Southern lady.

Now, the German and Spanish languages have harshness in their sounds. In other words, the Southerners came into Texas and said, "Hi, yawl." The Germans greeted them with "Guten Tag, wie geht's?" And the Spanish chimed in with a "Buenos tardes." Put that all together and you get, "Howdy!" The stridence of the Germanic language and the Hispanic speech coupled with the Southern drawl have created the Texas accent.

I'LL DO ANYTHING

People often ask me, "Just what is it you do, Rose-Mary?" I respond, "Anything!" Well, for many years I was a college professor, but now I primarily give speeches. "I talk," is my other answer. "Well, what do you talk about?" they ask. I respond, "Anything!"

I owe this current career to two ladies who really made a mark in the Dallas cultural and educational scene. One marvelous lady, Evelyn Oppenheimer, in the 1930s, a young girl just out of college, convinced Alex Sanger that he should offer book reviews each week at the Sanger Brothers auditorium. This review would bring ladies into the store and they would buy things. Spend money! Alex Sanger heard two words — spend money! After all, these were depression days, and if any money was spent, it was a miracle. Actually, if anyone had any money to spend, it was a miracle. So, Evelyn created the oral book review, and since then she has been reviewing books, writing books, and promoting books. She's a good speaker, she's a good writer, and she's a good agent. I heard Miss Oppenheimer in those days on the Sanger stage, and I admired her then, and I still admire her. I review books, I write books, and hopefully I promote books. I don't know how good I am, but I love doing what I'm doing. All of this reading has led me to other types of speaking, so after teaching for years, I fell into this marvelous career, thanks to Evelyn Oppenheimer.

There was another great lady who was definitely a part of my current career. This charmer was Ermance Rejebian.

Ermance, 14 years old, a native of Armenia, came to the United States. At this time, 1920, the Turks were killing the Armenians or driving them out of their country. Fortunately, Ermance escaped this horrible situation. She grew up and married Mr. Rejebian, a dealer in fine Persian rugs. The young couple came to Dallas in 1934. In 1936, Mrs. Rejebian attended a book review. The speaker chose to review, *The Forty Days of Musa Dagh*, a book about the Armenian tragedy. Mrs. Rejebian found flaws in the presentation, turned to her husband and expressed her displeasure. "Can you do better?" he asked. She was quick to respond, "Yes!"

The brilliant young lady decided to review books. But where would she get her audiences? Well, she created them! Mrs. Rejebian organized book clubs and the ladies and gentlemen who chose to join those clubs truly enjoyed their membership in them. There was a social hour and an hour of enlightenment. It was perfect. Those review clubs are active today all over the state. I was a speech teacher, so I had always given speeches. I was called upon to speak — but never considered doing just speeches. When I retired from teaching and counseling in 1982, I decided to speak and I've been talking ever since. I guess I'll go on as long as people ask me to speak and as long as the vocal chords hold out! Thank you Evelyn and Ermance!

A GODLY WOMAN?

Dr. W. A. Criswell, illustrious pastor of First Baptist Church, has always called me a "Godly woman." People have often asked me how I could supposedly be this spiritual person and also be involved in the theatre. "How do you do this?" they ask. My answer is, "Very carefully!" The modern theatre actually started in the church during the middle ages. Two monks spiced up the mass by reciting dialogue from the Bible. Everyone enjoyed it thoroughly. They were deeply moved by the reading. Then the monks began to write plays, again taking the dialogue straight out of the Bible. Then one monk strayed a bit. In the medieval drama entitled *Noah's Flood*, a priest took it upon himself to add a line. As Mrs. Noah was

33

getting on the ark, she turned to Noah and asked, "Can't we take a few neighbors?" This line was not in the scriptures. The priest who slipped in the line presented this argument on his behalf. "She probably did say it. Wouldn't you want some friends along if you knew you were going to be cooped up with Noah, the kids, and all those animals for 40 days and 40 nights?" Well, the argument didn't stand, so the theatre was tossed out of the church, and to this day the theatrical crowd doesn't always gel with the spiritual "godly" bunch.

Well, carefully, I taught theatre at Bishop Dunne High School, a very conservative Catholic school, and I also taught drama at Dallas Baptist University, a very conservative Baptist school. And in all seriousness, I will say that God truly blessed me in my work.

At Bishop Dunne, one year, I gave the play, *Harvey*, the story of Elwood P. Doud and his friend, a six foot rabbit named Harvey. The leading role of Elwood was played by a young man named Larry Pichard. Guess what? Larry today is a priest in the downtown parish, Lady of Guadalupe. To us old Dallasites, the grand structure on the corner of Ross and Pearl, will always be the Sacred Heart Cathedral. Nevertheless, Father Pichard is there holding high mass. His theatrical experience didn't ruin him spiritually.

When I was a Dallas Baptist, I directed my students in some religious productions. I offered these dramas to the churches. They could be given for special services. One of my greatest fans was the Reverend Tom Shipp who was at Lovers Lane Methodist Church when that church was actually located on Lovers Lane. Reverend Shipp loved my productions and often asked our group to come for a special program. His untimely death caused all of Dallas to grieve.

Father Harrison Lee, Rector at Christ Episcopal Church, has always appreciated my act. He's a very dramatic, enthusiastic man, so I appreciate his personality too. It's a mutual admiration. The members of this Episcopal church on 10th Street at Llewellyn, the first Episcopal church founded in Oak Cliff, are very fond of Father Lee.

I had a children's theatrical group at Dallas Baptist, and Reverend John Anderson, First Presbyterial Church, downtown, always invited us to come down and entertain the kids in vacation Bible school. I personally have always loved and appreciated Hans

34

Christian Andersen's story of the *Emperor's New Clothes*. I put the story into dramatic form and we gave it for the Presbyterian kids. If you remember, the Emperor's pride gets the best of him, and he finally ends up in a parade, marching through the town without clothes. My Emperor, Larry Horn, who is a drama professor today, was terrific in long red underwear. I assure you, he was well covered. Nevertheless, a little boy rushed out of vacation Bible school into his mother's waiting car, exclaiming, "Mama, Mama, we just saw the neatest play. This guy didn't have any clothes on." Oh, the hazards of theatre in the church.

I have such good friends in the Rowands, Dr. E. C., who was pastor of Central Christian Church on Westway, and his beautiful wife, Mary Louise. Their daughter, Diane, fabulous costumer, is married to Johnny Simons, founder, producer, writer, of the Hip Pocket Theatre in Fort Worth. So, the Rowands have theatrical ties. Dr. Rowand asked me to direct a play for their theatre group at the church, and from that play I established some life time friendships, one being with the Rowands.

One evening after a play at one of our local theatres, there was a party. The Rowands were there, and I was there with my mother who was about 87 at the time. There were two punch bowls at that party — one with and one without champagne. Mother always enjoyed refreshments. She was a tiny person, but she ate a lot — especially at parties. Well, before I knew it she had already gone through the punch line and I realized that this "alcohol has never touched my lips" person was drinking the punch laced with the bubbly. Oh, well, I decided, it wouldn't hurt her and knew for sure that it hadn't when she exclaimed, "Oh, my, this is the best Kool-Aid I've ever had." The Rowands, being extremely polite people didn't say anything, but I could tell they were giggling inside. Later, Dr. Rowand met me and asked about my mother. I told him that mother had died that year. His comforting words were, "Well, she's up in heaven drinking Kool-Aid." I shed a few tears over that sweet statement. We both did.

Today, Central Christian Church has a very talented pastor, Mike Waco. I was in some shows with Mike over at Casa Manana. He never mentions this to me when I see him, since he is now a man of the cloth.

My grandmother in 1879, was one of the founders of Zion

Lutheran Church. That first little church building was built on Swiss Avenue between Cantegral and Good Streets. One of the early pastors of that church was Ernest M. Robert. He was a kind and gentle man who preached two sermons on Sunday, one in English, the other in German. The German service was discontinued during and after World War II. Pastor Robert ministered to his little flock for many years. Then Pastor Carl Gaertner arrived on the scene. The church began to grow. There are several reasons why the congregation grew so rapidly. In the first place, Pastor Gaertner was a true evangelist and a good preacher. Secondly, after the war, many people came to Dallas from the North. There are more Lutherans in the North than in the South, so with this Northern influx, the church grew. Pastor Gaertner led the congregation to build a new church on the corner of Skillman and Lovers Lane where it stands today.

When my mother died, I wanted to present something to the church in her name. Pastor Gaertner and I discussed at length what would be the best thing for Mother and the church. We walked into the auditorium. It was complete except for a curtain on the stage. What better remembrance for my mother — a stage curtain for the church. How theatrical and spiritual can you get?

CHAPTER III

Some Stories
About the Area

WHY DALLAS?

John Neely Bryan was born in Lincoln County, Tennessee, December 10, 1810, of Scotch Irish Piedmont stock. His father was a prosperous farmer who gave to his boy what schooling was available. Nevertheless, at an early age, Bryan was on his own. He worked at the mill and studied at night. He read a course in law at Nashville where he received a license to practice law in Tennessee, and then he moved to Memphis. In 1833, not long after his arrival in Memphis, there was a severe epidemic of cholera and John was stricken with the disease. He thought that if he crossed into Arkansas and lived with the Indians there, he could strengthen his body. We really don't know much about Bryan at this time, but we do know that he emerged from his stay with the Indians knowing at least three different Indian languages. Obviously, he had contact with several different tribes.

Bryan grew tired of the primitive ways, and since he was well and strong now, he returned to white civilization where he took up a partner. The two men laid out the city of Van Buren, Arkansas, naming it after the President of the United States at that time.

It was there that Bryan heard of the rich and fertile land in Texas. The Indians that passed through Arkansas told of a village they established at Three Forks of the Trinity in land beyond the Red River. Bryan noticed that the Indians coming from the area seemed friendly, so off he went to seek the greener pastures. He stopped at Coffee's Trading Post. This was just over the Red River in Texas. In 1837, Holland Coffee and his bride left Washington-on-the-Brazos to travel north. They reached the Red River and settled there, opening this trading post. This little settlement later became known as Preston, Texas, named for Captain Preston, an officer in Colonel William G. Cooke's army. Colonel Cooke led his men northward from Austin to the Red River on a road that also would be named for Preston. The little town of Preston no longer exists. In fact, it's under Lake Texhoma. But Preston Road is alive and well traveled. Also, very alive is Preston Hollow, Preston Royal, Preston Forest, Prestonwood — the list is endless. I think it's funny that this name dominates a huge section of Dallas when this Captain Preston only passed here once and never even stopped. Good old Colonel Cooke has a county in the area named for him.

John Neeley Bryan arrived at the banks of the Trinity in 1839, but he soon returned to Van Buren. Nevertheless, he came back to Texas, and this time he stayed a little while. There had been two expeditions for the purpose of driving the Indians out. One was made by General E. H. Tarrant and the second by General James Smith. Smith rode to meet General Tarrant and passed by what was eventually to be Dallas. He camped at a spot just west of the Trinity where Oak Cliff is today. Smith found the remains of an Indian village in the Oak Cliff area which General Tarrant obviously had destroyed. It appeared that the area was fairly free of hostile Indians, so Bryan could easily start his little town.

Later when asked what he was going to name his little city, Bryan decided to go with the President's name as he had in Arkansas. The President was James K. Polk. Bryan could have blown it for Dallas right there. Polk is a nice name, but it just sort of sits there — Polk! It certainly would never have been a TV series — Polk! So Bryan went with the Vice-President, James Mifflin Dallas.

Now, I'm aware that there are other theories as to how Dallas got its name. Some say that only Dallas County bears the name of the Vice-President and that John knew someone named Dallas and chose to name the city after the friend. Some say he was too ignorant to even know who the Vice-President was. I still think that because he used a president's name in Arkansas, he was still thinking of the President when he was in Texas — or the Vice-President in this case. Who knows?????

When Texas went in as a state in 1845, everyone in Austin voted "yes" for statehood except one man. This man was Richard Bache, the grandson of Benjamin Franklin. He voted "No." Richard Bache was married to George Mifflin Dallas' sister. He had nine kids with her. He hated her, he hated the nine kids, he hated his brother-in-law, so he left Philadelphia, came to Texas, and voted "No" for statehood. They asked, "Why, Richard, why?" He replied. "Well, it's obvious. If anything happens to James K. Polk, the President, my idiot brother-in-law would be the President. We can't risk that!" Well, of course, Richard Bache was out-voted. Texas became a state. Later on, someone met Richard on the street in Austin and told him that a man in North Central Texas had named a city after his brother-in-law, Dallas. Richard had a stroke and dropped dead on the street in Austin. This man from Philadelphia is buried in the Oakwood Cemetery amid all of our Texas heroes. I say he rolled over in his grave every time the TV series came on named after his brother-in-law! Let's hope the reruns of the series do not disturb his rest too much!

EAGLE FORD

On November 11, 1989, a historical marker was placed at 2616 Chalk Hill Road, between Singleton and West Davis, to remember the once bustling town of Eagle Ford and its founders. The city came to be on the Trinity River at a shallow place — a ford. There just happened to be an eagle's nest hanging to the shore of the inlet — thus the name, Eagle Ford. Enock Horton and his family found the ford and the eagle. Enock was born in Virginia, but as a lad he moved with his parents to Springfield, Missouri. He married, had a family, and then came with his wife, seven girls, and three sons, in November, 1844, to Texas. He founded the little city on the Trinity.

Enoch was 67 years old when he arrived, so most of the development of the town was done by his son, James. This son married Jane Phillips, and the young couple soon opened a grist mill. They were later joined by Alexander Harwood and his family and then in 1881, by S. M. Luck and his son. Mr. Luck was also a miller. The population rose to 70 people. James Horton donated the land for the Texas Pacific Railroad to come through in 1874. With a cement plant built, the town was really booming. It looked like it would surpass the giant to the east, Dallas.

The cement plant, which opened in 1907, became the Portland Cement Company. The town was so large that it even had its own weekly newspaper, The *Weekly Eaglet*, which was run by W. W. Basaye. Eagle Ford was notorious for its fine bars, its great girls and the outlaws. This notoriety added to the business and glamour of this western town.

One of the most famous Eagle Ford landholders never lived there. At least 200 acres was owned by French Marshall Bazadine. Napoleon III sent him in the 1860s to set up Austrian Archduke Maximilian as the Emperor of Mexico. The Frenchman then acquired choice land in Eagle Ford. He never lived there, but he owned the land. There were some Frenchmen from La Reunion that spilled over into Eagle Ford. Part of the Santerre family was there. Eagle Ford continued to grow and eventually reached a population of 4,676 in 1940 when it was annexed into the city of Dallas. After World War II, many of the GIs and their families decided to live there. Houses couldn't be built fast enough, so there was a tent city built by the returning vets.

In 1955, the *Dallas Morning News* carried an interesting story of the Eagle Ford telegrapher, Byron A. Bates, who had been with the railroad since 1913. He was sending out messages as late as 1955. All those messages dealt with freight — not passengers.

One of the most famous railroad holdups of all time happened at Eagle Ford. This was when Sam Bass and his gang took on the train, April 4, 1878. Sam had come to Texas from Indiana — a Hoosier boy. When he was a kid, his mother died, his father remarried, so Sam became a wanderer. He spent some time in the Black Hills of South Dakota, and then later he wandered into Texas, Denton County to be exact. Here he took up with some pretty rough characters — Seaborn Brans, Thomas Spotswood, Arkansas Johnson (who happened to be from Missouri), Henry Un-

derwood, Sam Pips, and Albert Herndon. The only person who be-
friended him in Denton was Robert Caruth. "Old Bob" tried to
keep Sam on the straight and narrow, but failed.

Bob was the only person Sam ever called "Dad." Caruth had
hoped Sam and his gang would work around the Denton Area for
honest wages, but Sam and the outlaws had different ideas. They
could make so much more holding up trains. They had the whole
deal worked out perfectly. They called the gang the "Train Crew."
There was the conductor — Bass himself. There was the engineer.
This position was always up for grabs. Regardless, these train rob-
bers had it worked out to a science.

After robbing trains in Allen and in Hutchins, the next stop
for the Bass gang was Eagle Ford. The train left Dallas a few minutes after 11 P.M. on the 4th of April, 1878. There were four in the
gang — all masked. The ones that didn't go on the Eagle Ford job
were left holed up in Denton County. The depot agent had a gun,
but one man ordered him to toss it aside. He did. The take that
night was only $53 even though the mail car was robbed. Registered
mail didn't offer much loot. Bass and his bunch escaped. However,
eventually, Sam Bass was mortally wounded by a Texas Ranger in a
shoot out near Round Rock, Texas, July 21, 1878. Bass was only 27
years old when he died, but what a name he had carved for himself.

PETERS COLONY

Every morning an old lady came hobbling down Main Street
making her way to the Courthouse. She'd pass my grandfather's
bakery and my grandmother always invited her in for a cup of coffee and a donut.

Every day there was the same conversation. The old lady
would announce that she was on her way to the Courthouse to plead
her case. She claimed that she owned the property on which the
Courthouse stood, and she wanted the city to recognize that fact. She
claimed that she had the deed in her pocket. Since she came every
day, it was obvious that none of the judges listened to her. The
Courthouse VIPs considered her to be a nutty old lady with an in-
coherent story and obviously each day they shoved her aside. "Sure,
sure, old lady. Just sit here and wait." And she did!

Did that old lady really have the deed? Who knows? What we

41

do know is that the early property lines in the city were rather un-defined. In fact, when John Neely Bryan came back after one of his trips out of his little city, he wasn't sure if he still had his original property. Here's why.

In 1841, the Republic of Texas had problems. There was no money, and people were not pouring into the land as predicted — too many problems with the Indians. The tribes still weren't too friendly in some parts. The land was free for colonization, but with the fear of being scalped, who wanted the land? John P. Borden, head of the general land office, had all sorts of ideas about bringing people into Texas. There was a plan to bring 8,000 Frenchmen over, but the French didn't want to come. The biggest action to set-tle these parts was taken by William Smolling Peters. He offered 640 acres to any family or 320 acres to any single man who so de-sired to come to the wilds of Texas. These land claimers would be empressarios — set up Mexican fashion. Peters heard from people all over the United States and even people from England. Eventu-ally, he got almost 100 folks to go to Texas. He called this little band — Peters Colony.

W. S. Peters, an Englishman from Devonshire, who never bothered to become a United States citizen, arrived in Pittsburgh in 1820. There, he opened a music store. He sold pianos and gave piano lessons to his customers. He was hired to teach the children of Stephen Collins Foster, America's first composer. Later Peters moved to Cincinnati and began to publish music. Here he gained some fame as a composer himself and publisher of music. He pub-lished the songs of Stephen Collins Foster. In fact, Foster gave Pe-ters, as a gift, the song, "O SUSANNA." Peters published it and made $10,000 on it. Foster was a bit upset over this deal and men-tioned this to Peters who kindly sent Foster $100. Later, poor Fos-ter died on the street in Cincinnati almost penniless. In fact, the story goes that when his lifeless body was searched, only one penny was found in the pocket of his tattered coat.

Peters continued to wheel and deal. He opened a publishing company in Baltimore and eventually, 1829, moved to Louisville, Kentucky, where he opened another music store. But Peters didn't stop with music. He got into real estate. This is when he established Peters Colony with all of the promised land. Unfortunately, he laid out the plots with very blurred boundaries. That's why when the people got to this area, they also got into some very heated arguments over who owned what. Peters never came to Texas himself to help settle any of the disputes.

These indistinct boundaries created so much trouble for the members of Peters Colony, that many of these people just gave up on the original allotments and went off to seek and claim other land.

There was only one Englishman in the group, Daniel J. Carroll. He moved quickly and got his little town, Carrollton, started soon after his arrival.

With the railroad running northward in 1846, one stop was called Noell Junction. The postmaster was a Peter's Colony man, Addison Robertson. The name, Noell Junction, was dropped, and the little town was named Robertson. When the townspeople found that there was already a Robertson, Texas, the little town was then called Addison.

In 1846, the Peter's Colony bunch also moved southward. So often a new little town was named for a man who worked for the railroad. Such was the case of one village in the Southwest part of the Dallas area. The town was first called Duncan's Switch, for railroad man, Mr. Duncan. Now, it's Duncanville.

Dr. Daniel Rowlett of Peter's Colony went Eastward and established his little town. There was a Prussian in the crowd that also went Eastward with Dr. Rowlett. His name was William Sache. He first lived in New York, Philadelphia, and Missouri before coming to this area and establishing his little town.

Some of the people of Peters Colony moved Westward as was the case of Mr. Hurst, Mr. Euless, and Mr. Bedford. John Hurst in 1865 at first called his little town Hurst Springs. The Springs was later dropped.

Some of the colony people didn't go as far west, but remained in what is now Grapevine. Later, a group of folks from Missouri settled in Grapevine and established the first Baptist church in the area, Lonesome Dove Baptist Church. When the congregation first gathered, a dove lighted on the shoulder of the preacher, thus the name. Writer Larry McMurtry took the name of that Baptist Church and put it on a *bar* in his Pulitzer Prize winning novel, *Lonesome Dove.*

The Indians that these people met — Wacos and Shawnee — were fairly peaceful. There were no Indian battles — only battles

43

over the property lines. That was why Bryan didn't have his original claim. His land was given away by Peters.

Mr. Peters, by the way, died of heart disease in Louisville, April 20, 1866. He died while writing a song of the promised land, "Jerusalem, the Golden."

Could that old lady, with that supposed deed in her pocket, have been part of the original Peters Colony? Who knows? Nevertheless, she enjoyed her coffee and a donut every morning with my grandmother!

STREETS!

By 1844, John Neely Bryan's little trading post, Dallas, had some well-marked and well-named streets. John himself named these Dallas streets: Houston, Lamar, Jefferson, Jackson, Polk, Sycamore, Columbia, Main, Commerce, and Market. It's fairly obvious where he acquired these names — Presidents, Texas heros, a tree, Americana. Sycamore and Polk Streets were both downtown. They eventually vanished from the downtown area, but there is today a Sycamore in East Dallas and a Polk in Oak Cliff.

However, there were two streets (one does not exist today) that John named for Frenchmen — Poydras and Carondelet. Julien de Lalande Poydras was a Frenchman who came from Brittany to New Orleans in 1768. He acquired a great amount of money and shared it with the people. Baron Francisco Luis Hector Carondelet served as the Governor of Louisiana and also of West Florida in 1791. Carondelet is the street that doesn't exist anymore. It was absorbed by Ross Avenue. Nevertheless, the questions stands. Why did John name these streets after these particular Frenchmen? The only logical explanation comes with the fact that John Neely Bryan and his buddy, Captain Mabel Gilbert, who was a steamboat master on the Mississippi, lived in New Orleans together for a while before Bryan came to Texas. Our founder could have remembered some good times that he had on those two streets, Poydras and Carondelet, in New Orleans. That's the best explanation. By the way, John never named a street for himself. Bryan Street was named after his death.

In 1872, there were some new streets and some new names. John Henry Brown, Street Commissioner, met with his council and came up with these names.

Hord Street was named for W. H. Hord, who settled with his family in 1845, west of the Trinity.

Cochran Street was named for William M. Cochran, first County Clerk of Dallas, 1846.

Harwood Street was named for Alexander Harwood, County Clerk, 1850–51, 1875–83. He walked from Shreveport to Dallas in 1842.

Patterson Street was named for J. M. Patterson, first general merchant in Dallas, 1846. He was later a County Judge.

Good Street was named for John J. Good, lawyer, landowner, and Mayor of Dallas, 1880–81.

Burford Street was named for N. M. Burford, a lawyer who arrived in Dallas in 1848 and declared that there were only twelve males in town then. Later, as a judge, Burford addressed an angry mob during an uprising after the Civil War. Still later, in 1872, he made the speech to welcome the railroads into Dallas.

Crockett Street was named for John M. Crockett, early lawyer, 1848 and later Mayor in 1860.

Martin Street was named for Bennett H. Martin, District Judge, 1848–1850.

Field Street was named for Tom Field who built the first Opera House in Dallas.

Ervay Street was named for the Mayor Henry S. Ervay, who was admired when he chose to go to jail rather than to carry out the orders of the reconstructionists in 1870.

Ross Avenue was named for William and Andrew Ross, ex-wine merchants who owned the land on both sides of the street.

Wood Street was named for George T. Wood, Governor of Texas, 1848. He was admired by the common man because he rode a mule.

There were some streets that had name changes. In 1917, at the start of World War I, Germania Street was changed to Liberty. Just before World War II, Lindbergh Boulevard was changed to Skillman Avenue. Lindy has fallen out of favor with the country for his sympathy for the German people. W. F. Skillman, a Dallas banker, was president and general manager of Prudential Building and Loan Association.

After World War II, General Walton Walker was honored with a street named for him. General Walker, commander of the

45

36th Texas Infantry Division, led his troops, known as the Ghost Corps. They acquired this title for their swift and sudden knockout operations against the Germans.

In Dallas, the big question remains — who was Harry Hines? He was an oil man and civic leader, born in 1886, died in 1954. On June 24, 1956, the large thoroughfare was named for him. Mr. Hines, who served as Chairman of the Texas Highway Commission from 1935 to 1941, was appointed to this position by Governor Jimmy Alred. While Hines served on this board, he saw the need for a new route to run northwest out of Dallas. When that route was finally completed, the city council named this street after him.

STREETS!

The illustrious, dynamic, and Bible totin' preacher of the First Baptist Church, Dallas, Wally Amos Criswell, always worked fervently to eliminate liquor from the face of the earth. He especially didn't want alcohol around the First Baptist Church Complex which stands on St. Paul, Ross, Ervay, and Federal Streets. For years, there was a package store in the Cotton Exchange Building on St. Paul, right across the street from the church. Dr. Criswell, after years of prayer and spiritual actions, forced the proprietor to move his liquor store elsewhere. In 1982, when the church sold some property on Ervay Street across from the church, a promise was made — no alcohol will be served *on* Ervay Street. The Dakota Restaurant is underground. Alcohol is served *under* Ervay Street. How about that for a religious loop hole?

Nevertheless, First Baptist Church does stand on a very ethereal sounding street — St. Paul, named for the agressive, first century missionary. This is quite proper for the church — but is it? What is the story behind the street's name? St. Paul Street was named by Barnett Gibbs, who served as Lieutenant Governor of the State of Texas from 1884 to 1886. Gibbs was a staunch anti-prohibitionist. He certainly was not an alcoholic, but he loved to take a nip — a big nip — now and then, and he thought it was perfectly all right to do so. In fact, he felt that it was a healthy thing to do. So, when Gibbs built the street in front of his house, he wanted to name that street in honor of the author of these words he found so inspirational. "Drink no longer water, but use a little wine for thy stomach's sake." St. Paul wrote those words, I Timothy 5:23, Holy Bible. So the name was given to the street in honor of the author, St. Paul. Now, all you tee totalers, think not harshly of Paul. After all, he spoke of this wine only for medicinal purposes!

The real spiritual story lies with Young Street. That street was named for the Reverend William C. Young, a Confederate Missionary Chaplain, who became a Dallas preacher and politician after the Civil War. Marilla was named for Young's wife. Canton was the name of Young's birthplace in Trigg County, Kentucky. Cadiz was the Trigg County seat. Some Dallas citizens thought Cadiz was named for a city in Spain, so during the Spanish-American War, some wanted the name changed. Finally, it was revealed that the name came from Kentucky.

The suburb of Oak Cliff went with the Presidents for street names. This all started when John Neely Bryan named one of the major thoroughfares, Jefferson. This street led into Oak Cliff, so it was natural for other Presidents to be honored. When Oak Cliff merged with Dallas in 1903, Washington Street was changed to Zang Boulevard in honor of John F. Zang, an Oak Cliff developer.

Some Oak Cliff streets were named by Leslie Stemmons. While Stemmons was studying law in Chicago, he became very enamored of Winnetka, a fashionable suburb on Lake Michigan. When Stemmons developed Winnetka Heights in 1908, he named the streets for their counterparts in Illinois — Edgefield, Windomere, Rosemont, Montclair, and Willomet.

In 1908, there was a flood and Dallas was completely under water. Stemmons decided he could tame the river, so he created from the river bottoms what was called the Industrial District. Unfortunately, he died in 1939 and did not live to see his dream realized. Nevertheless, his sons, John and Leslie Storey, continued the development and named the streets. First, they decided that they would name the streets after trees. However, Dallas seemed to have enough "tree" streets, so he settled for some fairly unusual names. Dragon Street came from a conversation one of the brothers had with his wife. "They're draggin' in the work — just draggin'." The street was named Dragon. Hi Line was named for the nearby power line. Glass was named for Pittsburgh Plate Glass. Harvester, of course, came from International Harvester. And Continental was named for the Continental Bus Line. Stemmons wanted to name

47

Slocum Street for Joe Slocum Electric Company, but there was sort of an unwritten rule — no streets could be named for people who were alive. So Stemmons sent his staff members to search for a namesake — a bogus namesake. They found one in General Henry Warner Slocum, a Yankee. Thus, Slocum Street got its name in spite of the rule.

AND MORE STREETS!

Barnes Bridge Road. A toll bridge across the East Fork of the Trinity was operated by R. Barnes.

Dowdy Ferry. Alasan Dowdy operated a ferry to cross the river near Hutchins.

Record Crossing. George W. Record's gristmill was used by the people of Irving.

Military Parkway. This was the way to Peacock Military Academy which is now Urban Park Elementary School.

Buckner Boulevard. R. C. Buckner was the founder of the Orphan's Home over 100 years ago.

Bruton Road. Richard Bruton was a Pleasant Grove pioneer who settled 320 acres in the 1840s.

Greenville Avenue. This was the road to Greenville, Texas.

McKinney Avenue. This was the road to McKinney, Texas, a city which was named for Collin McKinney, the oldest man to sign the Texas Declaration of Independence, 1836.

Scyene Road. This was the road to Scyene, Texas, named for an ancient Egyptian city. Outlaw Belle Starr was a well known resident of Scyene.

Cedar Springs Road. This was the road to Cedar Springs, Texas. This little town was almost named the county seat of Dallas County.

Kiest Boulevard. Edwin J. Kiest was the publisher of the *Dallas Times Herald* for 45 years. He gave the land for Kiest Park.

Samuell Boulevard. Dr. W. W. Samuell was a prominent doctor in Dallas who just happened to have delivered me!

Royal Lane. Royal A. Ferris, Jr. was a co-owner of the Browning-Ferris Machinery Company. He had a country place out on the lane.

Josey Lane. Colonel Clint Josey was an oil man in Dallas. His wife had a rare book collection. I purchased several of her books when they were auctioned to the public.

Coit Road. John Taylor Coit trained Confederate recruits at Trinity Mills, a town near Carrollton.

Gus Thomasson Road. Gus Thomasson was the district director of the Works Progress Administration during the 30s.

Marvin D. Love. Mr. Love was branch manager for the Dallas Power and Light in Oak Cliff.

Marsh Lane. Thomas C. Marsh killed the last buffalo east of the Trinity.

Webbs Chapel Road. Isaac and Mary Webb came to Texas in 1842 from Missouri. They were so impressed with the land that they road all the way back to Missouri to tell their friends about it. They returned to settle here.

Peak Street. Captain Jefferson Peak operated a steam boat between Cincinnati and New Orleans. He moved to Dallas in 1854 with his five sons, Carroll, Junius, Worth, Victor and Wallace.

Akard Street. William Christopher Columbus Akard moved to Dallas from North Carolina, a state that was destroyed by the Civil War.

Haskell Avenue. Horatio Haskell was Alderman of East Dallas in the 1880s. He fought with Zachary Taylor in the Mexican War, and he also went on the 10 man expedition of the Platte River. Most of this group froze to death. Haskell made it, returned, and settled in Dallas.

Belmont Avenue. August Belmont, a New York financier, developed the Belmont area just before he went broke in the crash of 1893.

Cantagrel Street. Francois Jean Cantagrel was head of the La Reunion Colony Company.

Forney Avenue. John W. Forney, Philadelphia newspaperman, was the publicity agent for the Texas and Pacific Railroad when it rolled into Dallas in 1872.

Lamar Street. Mirabeau B. Lamar was the second president of the Texas Republic. Every large city in Texas has a Lamar Street.

Lemmon Avenue. W. N. Lemmon was a land developer.

Parry Avenue. W. E. Parry, early resident of the area, served as City Secretary, 1884–87.

Routh Street. Rev. Jacob Routh was a pioneer Dallas preacher.

Some of the Dallas streets have Indian names. Some were named right after World War I. These were Versailles, Belleau, Argone, Bordeaux, and Lausanne. Oddly enough, there was a Rhine Street.

LA REUNION

H. L. Hunt, billionaire oil man, who at one time was the richest man in the world, came to Dallas and gave the city some added identity — a city with a lot of money. Ray Hunt, his son and Dallas developer, has contributed more identity to the city. This time to the skyline. Ray built Reunion Tower — the big lighted ball. When I was a kid, the Dallas skyline was known by the flying red horse. Today, Dallas is identified by that ball. When Ray developed that area, he named it Reunion — Reunion Tower, Reunion Hyatt Regency, Reunion Arena. La Reunion was the name given to the little French colony of people who attempted to establish a Utopia in Dallas in 1855, but failed. Ray Hunt chose to honor these people.

During the last half of the eighteenth century, France experienced a revolution which reverberated throughout Europe. The French Revolution turned into a blood bath which was followed by a situation that proved to be even worse. A little Emperor, Napoleon, seized control, and France and really all of Europe fell into mad chaos. People were looking for relief. There must be a way to rebuild the crumbling ruins of the past. But how? Philosophers were seeking ideas that could be put into action that would end all poverty and misery. Most of these European philosophers truly felt that the solution of the economic ills would come when there was a guarantee of equitable distribution of wealth to the masses of people. This new proposed system became known as Socialism. The concentration of wealth must be destroyed. Money in the hands of just a few could be prevented if production and distribution of goods and services could remain in control of the people who produced the materials and services in the first place. Could social and economic development occur when all inequality and special privileges were eliminated from the political and economic life? The Socialists thought so.

Francois Fourier, French Philosopher, declared that misery,

50

poverty, and unhappiness came from suppression of natural desires and passions. All that was needed for perfect harmony in a social life was the development and satisfaction of natural desires. Here was his plan. He would organize a colony of people with everyone working for that colony. Whenever one form of labor or association became monotonous for the individual, he could easily transfer to another type of work or to another group of associates and everyone would live happily ever after. Fourier had an opportunity to test out his scheme in 1833 in France. The society was founded but members could not agree on the work, so the whole thing collapsed. Fourier literally died with a broken heart, but nevertheless, one of his followers, Victor Prosper Considerant, still believed the idea would work. Considerant left for the United States, November 28, 1852, to find a suitable place for his colony. He toured the whole Eastern part of the country and finally drifted down to Preston, the city on the Red River — the border town between Oklahoma and Texas. Considerant was impressed by the beauty of the land and the rich soil, so he decided that the little colony, La Reunion, would operate in Texas. His people got together in France, wrote out the constitution, and sailed for America, eventually arriving in Dallas, June 16, 1855. They settled on the South side of the Trinity River because of the hills, the valleys, the cliffs, and the Oaks. The area was appropriately called Oak Cliff.

When Considerant visited Texas the first time, he had been well received. People encouraged him to come. But when these Socialists actually arrived, it was a different story. The *Texas Gazette* reported, "We are always pleased to have industrious immigrants come among us. However, we note this advent of Socialism in Texas as forboding us no good; and we wish them to have a fair understanding that as a political sect, our whole people are against them."

Nevertheless, the people of La Reunion began to build their houses. By April 1856, they had homes, a building for making soap and candles, a laundry, a building for offices, a kitchen, a grocery store, beehives, a chicken house, a smoke house, a forge. At first sight of the village, a visitor might think that all was fine and dandy. But it wasn't. The whole idea was doomed from the start. The households began to break up into their own private enterprises. There was some dishonesty among the crowd. Some were

51

just not able to do certain things when it came their time. They were experts in just certain fields. They couldn't swap jobs. Then too, Considerant chose Francois Jean Cantagrel as the leader, and he wasn't strong enough to hold the thing together. Most of the Frenchmen returned home, but a few stayed — Jacque Maximillien Reverchon and family, August Guillot and family, Francois Santerre and family, Francois Considerant and family — to name a few. These people stayed and prospered as capitalists in Dallas.

THOSE PROSPEROUS SUBURBS
HAD RATHER HUMBLE BEGINNINGS

In 1846, a little village was founded by William Foreman. When people came to the area, they asked the name. "Foreman," was the reply. "What's that? You named a town after *Fillmore*, that Yankee president?" Southerners hated President Fillmore. A group suggested the Spanish name for "plain" be used. This would be "llano." There was already a Llano, Texas, so the group substituted that first L for a P — Plano.

I remember when I was a kid, Plano was just a little farming community. I also remember that we took Grandma's feather beds out to Plano to be made into comforts. That priceless down from Eider ducks, that soft plumage under the feathers, was recycled and put into gorgeous comforts. The Alden Comfort Mill is still very much in business today, but they make more than comforts. Plano is much more than farming and feathers today. It's probably one of the most prosperous areas in the metroplex.

Another wealthy and elite community in the metroplex had rather humble beginnings. In 1858, when the town was founded, the vice-president under Buchanan was John C. Breckenridge. A little town north of Dallas was named for him. There was already a Breckenridge, Texas, so the little town was renamed for a railroad man, Richardson.

Minister Allen came to the area and established a little town which he wanted to name after his home town in Michigan — Pontiac. There was already a Pontiac, Texas, so he went with another Michigan name — Saginaw.

The underground rock formation on the eastern side of our county prompted the name of Rockwall. This little town had a jitney service to and back from Dallas. Mr. R. A. Gaines bought a Maxwell car for $1,475. He carried folks into and back from Dallas daily for $10, round trip.

J. F. Green settled in Collin County, and when his little girl was born, he named the little town north of McKinney after this first child, Anna.

In 1850, there was a horse race in a little village east of Dallas. A man won the race with a canter. The people holding the race decided to name the little village after the canter. The problem came when they couldn't spell canter. The town is named Canton.

Going eastward toward Lake Lavon, there was a group of people who settled together. One individual exclaimed, "I don't have a nickel in my pocket." The little town was called Nickleville. When the railroad came in, 1886, the engineer, Colonel W. D. Wylie, decided that the town should be named for him. After all, he was in charge of the train. It was no longer Nickleville. It was Wylie.

The town of DeSoto was founded in 1848. It was originally named The Store, because T. J. Johnson had a store — simple as that. In 1881, a Dr. Thomas Hernando DeSoto Stewert officially gave the town one of his middle names — DeSoto. So the town really wasn't named for the Spanish explorer but for a man whose mother obviously honored the explorer by naming her son for him.

WHO IS IRVING?

A Jewish friend of mine has always chortled over the fact that there is a city in Texas named Irving. "Who is Irving? Irving Levine? Irving Berlin? Who is this Irving?"

In 1880, a little city called Gorbett was established west of the Trinity just where the Chicago, Rock Island, and Gulf Railroad was to run. Thomas C. Storey was the postmaster. When the railroad didn't go in the direction that was proposed, the little city of Gorbett moved. Actually, this little city really never got a good start, so it eventually disappeared. In 1902, J. O. Schulze and Otis Brown promoted another site on the railroad. Mrs. Brown loved reading the novels of Washington Irving, so she asked her husband to honor her favorite writer and name the little town Irving. Writer Washington Irving was born near Plymouth Rock, thus there is a shopping center in Irving named Plymouth Park.

53

Irving grew steadily through the first half of the twentieth century, and by 1940, there were 1,089 people living in the little city. Most of the men worked for the railroad. After World War II, like most of Texas and the nation, Irving grew rapidly. Plants that produced paint, cement, and aluminum products opened. There was mill work. Roofing supplies were produced along with chemical supplies. Soon there were over one thousand businesses in Irving, Texas, with companies dealing in petroleum products and electronic components also sprang up. And then to top it all off, the area had John W. Carpenter.

This hustling giant, John W. Carpenter, was born on a farm near Corsicana, August 31, 1881. He was one of ten children. John first went to rural county schools and later attended North Texas Normal in Denton and Draughan's Business College in Dallas. His first job was on a farm. Later he went to work for an implement supply company. Then he began to dig post holes for the Corsicana Gas and Electric Company. From digging holes he went on to become a lineman. From the lineman's job he moved on to be an engineer. In 1905, he was sent to New York and Ohio to serve in various positions with the power companies. He went back to Corsicana in 1913 to be general manager of the power and light company there. By 1918, he was appointed general manager of the Dallas Power and Light. Twenty-five major power companies were organized under his guidance. Carpenter served as president of the Dallas Chamber of Commerce and also president of the State Fair of Texas. In 1930 he worked diligently with the Trinity Improvement Association. He was a large man who believed in hard work. His story is one of success — from digging holes to heading the corporate office.

In 1928, Mr. Carpenter acquired his ranch which he called Hackberry Creek. Mrs. Carpenter didn't think the name was very romantic, so she insisted that the land be called El Ranchito de las Colinas, the little ranch in the hills.

On September 14, 1970, John's son, Ben, and son-in-law, Dan Williams, presented a master plan for a mega-business and residential complex. There would be a country club with adjoining luxury homes. There would be a canal running through the whole scene with boats to take people from business to business — from shop to shop. This all came to pass with much more — a communications center with a movie sound stage comparable to anything in Hollywood. Many production companies now office in this complex.

Hundreds of people go to see the sculpture — "The Mustangs" — at Williams Square. The nine bronze horses stand one-and-one half times larger than life. They seem to move through the water in the fountain there in the midst of two acres of granite and concrete. Heaven only knows how many pictures have been taken of this art created by sculptor Robert Glen of South Africa.

Last, but certainly not least, Irving, Texas, in 1970, got Texas Stadium with Tom Landrey and the Dallas Cowboys! So, who is Irving? Well, it's a city with a lot going for it.

CEDAR HILL

Cedar Hill, the highest point in Dallas County, once a stop on the Chisholm Trail, was the county seat of Dallas County from 1846 to 1848. Alexander Hart, J. M. Williams, and William C. Hart were men who all figured in the founding of this quaint little town. Another early settler was Crawford Trees, who came from Illinois in 1845 and married Anna Minerva Kimmell. They were issued the first marriage license in Dallas County. Mr. Trees went to California in 1849 and returned in two years with several thousand dollars worth of gold. By 1883, he was the largest landowner in the county. His land reached into the town of Duncanville.

From Missouri came Samuel and Salinda Ramsey with their son, Jesse. Little Jesse went to a driftfloor schoolhouse at Ten Mile Creek, where a professor Scott rigidly taught the kids. James Horton came in 1857 and opened the first mill in the county. In 1848, J. W. Holland came from Illinois and made the small village his home.

With these people came early industry. Since there was no barbed wire fencing yet, the cedars which were so plentiful in the area were cut and used for fencing timbers. By 1856, there was a blacksmith shop, a post office, and a store, Miller and Berry. And, of course, the Methodists built a beautiful little church with a bell tower. This church was founded in 1854 with 150 members. T. J. Felkner was the pastor.

Now, all was going well for these people in their little hamlet, but unfortunately, disaster struck. At 3 P.M., April 29, 1856, a tornado swept through Cedar Hill blowing the entire town away and killing 11 citizens. The winds were so strong that a piece of silk from the Miller Berry Store was found 20 miles away in Cedar Springs. A hat box from the store was found at White Rock Lake, 30 miles away. A large plow was blown a half mile from the store. This natural disaster was certainly devastating, but the people of Cedar Hill determinedly rebuilt their town.

These people helped in the rebuilding. Dr. Rufus A. Roberts, a graduate of Jefferson Medical College in Philadelphia, arrived in Cedar Hill in 1859. He first practiced medicine in Marion, North Carolina. In 1861, Dr. Roberts served as a surgeon in the Confederate army. After the war he returned to Cedar Hill and served the community as doctor and pharmacist. He was also instrumental in getting the railroad into the town. The line from Cleburne was finished in 1882. Later, Dr. Roberts was a delegate to the first Democratic state convention which was held in Galveston.

Mr. Charles Straus started out in Cedar Hill as a door to door salesman, but he finally acquired enough money to open his store, a popular spot in the community. As more and more people arrived there was more and more demand for various retail markets. Mr. S. P. Lovern had a candy store, but really he sold almost everything. Mr. Vesta Bennett had a drug store. Mrs. Brooks Roberts owned and operated the hotel. The food she served was outstanding. Still another drug store specializing in sodas and sundaes was opened by J. C. Potter. When electricity became available, the city was lighted by the Dynamo Electric Plant. Lights blinked at 10:30 P.M. every evening and then the town was plunged into total darkness at 11 P.M. Everyone then went to sleep peacefully in the dark silent little village of Cedar Hill.

H. A. GARLAND, POSTMASTER

Mr. Ray Campbell, who is part of the public information staff of our Dallas County Community Colleges, was a former student of mine. Now, he's a dear friend with whom I often swap "good ole" Dallas stories. His father, Ray Campbell, was a very well known insurance man in Dallas, but actually Ray's roots go back to the very beginning of Dallas County.

His great-great-great grandfather, a Kentucky Colonel,

Thomas Jefferson Nash, settled in the area which is now Garland, Texas. In 1851, Nash came to look the place over, then he went back to Kentucky, and then he came back in 1853 to build his home. His farm was around the LBJ/Saturn area.

Sam Houston, in 1860, appointed Colonel Nash to the office of County Commissioner. In 1861, the old Kentucky Colonel was definitely in favor of the Confederacy, so he went to Austin to campaign for secession. Sam Houston did not want Texas to join the Confederacy. He wanted Texas to once again become a nation, a republic, as it had been under his presidency. Sam hoped that Texas then would stay out of the war, stand alone, and just watch the North and the South scrap it out. He felt that Texas should not get involved. Well, Texas seceded, and Colonel Nash was on the committee that was there in Austin to see that it did. When Texas joined the Confederacy, Sam Houston resigned as Governor and went home to die of a broken heart. T. J. Nash went on living to support the South. He, more of less, betrayed the man who appointed him a Commissioner.

After the war, Thomas Jefferson Nash became the father of a couple of boys, one being T. F. Nash, who was to become a county judge in Dallas and then a district judge in the state. All this time, other families began arriving in the area known now as Garland. In fact, enough families arrived to start two little towns — Duck Creek, obviously named for a creek with a duck on it, and Embree, named for Dr. K. H. Embree, who also settled in the area. As the two little cities began to grow, they were both hoping for a post office. This would make them real little towns, not just gatherings. A fight arose over which one should have the post office. T. F. Nash, a real politician, suggested that the two towns get together, form one town, and name it after the Postmaster General of the United States. When this postmaster would hear that a town was named for him, he'd be so excited that he'd arrange for a post office. The Post Master General at this time, under President Grover Cleveland, was H. A. Garland.

Before T. F. Nash became a judge he was the editor of the original Mesquite newspaper, *The Texas Mesquiter*. Later, he moved to Dallas and lived in a grand old house on Routh Street, which now houses a darling store, The Sample House. By the way, the Rouths were an old Garland family.

Judge Nash had many stories which he gathered while sitting on the bench. There was the one about old Sam. It seemed that Sam was in Judge Nash's court pleading for mercy. "Now, you know, Judge, my wife just died, and I'm in terrible trouble."

"Sam," said the Judge, "I believe I heard this story last year. I believe your wife died last year."

"Yeah," Judge, "I just can't keep a wife noways!" Case dismissed!

By the way, my son married a good Garland girl, Karen Stevens. Her parents, Lewis and Juanita Stevens, have been residents of Garland for a number of years.

THE MIDCITIES

There's always been a lot of action in the midcities. Where Arlington stands today, in 1831, General Edward H. Tarrant authorized Jonathan Bird to establish a fort so that the few very early settlers who had survived in the area would have some protection from the Indians. The settlement was called Birds Fort. Then in 1838, Captains Robert Sloan and Nathaniel T. Journey led a group of 90 frontiersmen on an expedition against the Indians in the same area. Eventually, General Tarrant and General George W. Terrell met with 9 tribes of Indians at Birds Fort to settle the boundaries between the Republic of Texas and Indian lands.

With the Santa Fe Trail running through the region, more and more people began to settle in the area. In 1842, Middleton Tate Johnson arrived and called his little town Johnson Station. Later, James Ditto renamed Johnson Station, Arlington. He said the land was so beautiful that it reminded him of Arlington, Virginia. Mr. Randol opened a mill, and things began to blossom.

A little to the east, Alexander Deckman, in 1865, settled and named his little village Deckman, obviously after himself. Later, as the land developed the people pointed out that they were living on the grandest of all prairies, so the town of Decker became known as Grand Prairie.

These midcities together were destined to become the entertainment capital of the world. W. T. Waggoner, oil and cattle man, who, when he died in 1934, had the largest individual fortune in the world, built, in 1933, Arlington Downs. Waggoner loved horses, parimutuel betting was legal in the State, so the track was built. Bettin' Texans enjoyed that race track from 1933 to 1937. Then parimutuel betting was declared illegal, so the races came to a halt. The structure stood until 1958. Various activities, such as square dance festivals, were held at the Downs, but gambling was out!

In the late 50s Angus G. Wynne, Jr. began the construction of a theme park which he decided to name after the Six Flags of Texas. There would be 6 sections in the park — one for each flag that flew over our state — Spanish, French, Mexican, Texas Republic, United States, and Confederate. Wynn called upon the old showman, Charlie Meeker, to help him with the project. Charlie had been the producer of the Dallas Summer Musicals until Tom Hughes took over. Well, the park opened in 1957, and it's been growing ever since.

When I was teaching at Dallas Baptist University, I sent several drama students to audition for the shows at Six Flags. Many got really great summer jobs out of the deal. One big guy, Randy Newberry, who today is a Baptist foreign missionary, one summer, was a gun slinger in the Frontier Days show. He came back to tell the drama class that he was going to be shot at least 48 times a day. Quite an adventure! I'm sure this experience has proven time and time again to be helpful in his present work on the mission field.

Sports have always played a big part in the midcities. In 1965, Turnpike Stadium was built for the Dallas-Fort Worth Spurs. The city of Arlington bought the stadium in 1969 and the Texas Rangers are now at home there. But not for long. Arlington is looking forward to a new stadium that will prevail over the city.

WHY MESQUITE?

Mesquite owes its existence to Warren Angus Ferris and John and James Beeman. Ferris, a surveyor and adventurer, gave the final word as to where the Peters Colony group would settle and where those who had already come to Dallas County could remain. Then in 1843, John Beeman with his brother, James, arrived on the scene. They claimed the land in and around White Rock. By 1850,

White Rock Creek had a post office which was established by James Beeman. Later, the post office was called Prairie Creek, and then for some reason, it was called Scyene. The name Scyene came out of Egyptian history. The word means "key" or "opening." In 1873, when the railroad arrived, east of the town of Scyene a depot was established. It was called Mesquite, named for the trees in the area.

CHAPTER IV

Some Dallas Firsts

DALLAS' FIRST PHONE CONVERSATION

At the Philadelphia Centennial Exposition, 1876, people picked up the new invention offered by Alexander Graham Bell for the first time and exclaimed, "It talks!" This Exposition, which displayed many remarkable inventions, was still dominated by the most dramatic creation of all, the telephone.

The first phone in Dallas, or I should say, the first two phones in Dallas, (What good could come from one phone?) were installed at Browder Springs (Old City Park) and the water works, downtown. This communicational set up was good news for the Dallas Fire Department, because the water company could then instantly communicate with the pump station and get more water for fires.

On May 15, 1881, the first business in Dallas put in a phone. This was at J. M. Oram's Jewelry Store, 222 Elm Street.

When Oram connected with Central he was told not to say anything until he heard something. When he heard the voice from Central he was so excited that he ran out onto Elm Street shouting in amazement.

The next business phone to go in was at Apperson's Drug

Store, Main and Poydras. Uncle Jake Smith, an old timer who hung around the drug store, wouldn't believe that Oram was talking to Apperson. "Someone is behind that partition," Uncle Jake pointed out. When the gang at the drug store showed him that no one was near, Uncle Jake was truly speechless that Oram could be heard from such a distance.

Col. John C. McCoy, put in a phone at his home on Commerce and Lamar. He had this to say about it all. "I always feel that everyone in the world is hearing me. It's like the voice of a ghost."

By June 1881, there were forty phones in Dallas. Long distance was installed, August 2, 1881. The lines went to Lancaster first and then to Waxahachie. In 1881, long distance went to Midlothian. Later, this line had to be redone, because the people in Midlothian kept getting the people in Lancaster. What fun!

When I was growing up in the depression, we all had party lines. If we kids didn't have anything to do, we could always listen in on the neighbor's conversation. It was quite easy to fall out of friendship with a neighbor over the line. I remember the lady across the alley from us hated me and my friends, because we translated our Latin assignments on the phone. This took hours.

Investing in Bell was a good move from the very start. The first million dollars capital came in 1879. The first million dollars of earning was in 1882. A Dallasite, Royal A. Ferris, decided to invest in the system in 1881. When his father heard that his son was going to invest, the father had a doctor sent to see if the son was insane. Ferris decided not to invest and lost a quarter of a million dollars almost over night.

THE ELEVATOR

In a style not quite as flamboyant as P. T. Barnum, Elisha Otis on May 1, 1854, hoisted himself up on a platform over an ogling crowd that stood at New York's Crystal Palace. He rose up on the platform that was pulled by a rope wound around a power driven drum. When Otis was high, high, high above the crowd, he cut the rope. The crowd screamed. The platform fell a couple of inches and stayed in place. The crowd then cheered. He had introduced a safe elevator.

There are two buildings in Dallas that boast of having the first passenger elevator. You be the judge.

FIRST ELEVATOR #1

One of the oldest skyscrapers in Dallas is the Wilson Building on the corner of Elm, Ervay, and Main. H. L. Green's, variety store, occupies the area now. This building, constructed in 1904 by J. B. Wilson, was patterned after the spectacular and prodigious French Opera House built in Paris by Napoleon. The Wilson Building of eight stories was magnificent. Notice I used the past tense — *was*. The sculptured pillars have been covered by the ugliest front imaginable.

Now, please understand, I have nothing against H. L. Greens. I love H. L. Greens. It's a great retail store — one of the few left in downtown Dallas. I just hate the added store front. Hideous material was wrapped around the gorgeous pillars. The present front is just not in keeping with the grandeur that was once part of that building.

When the building was opened, it had solid mahogany doors and woodwork that was considered the best in the world. There were marble floors. Here is a direct quote from the media on the day the building was dedicated. "Dallas may justly claim to have the largest and the most convenient and most up-to-date business and office building in the South. The Wilson Building is the aristocrat among business blocks." At that time there was only one building that came close to being what the Wilson Building was. This building housed Marshall Field in Chicago. Many architects declared the Dallas building the grandest of all.

The creator, J. B. Wilson, was born in 1847, in Toronto, Canada. He decided to seek his fortune in the United States, so at age 18 years, he left his home for New Orleans. Eventually, he made his way to Dallas in 1872. He had been in the lumber business in Louisiana, so he decided to stick with lumber when he came to Texas.

The Wilson Lumber Company was quite profitable. In fact, it was so profitable that Mr. Wilson was able to buy a second home — a ranch near San Angelo. With lumber and cattle, he amassed a fortune. Later, Wilson served on the board of directors of City National Bank. He acted as treasurer of the Tiche-Goettinger Store. This was quite appropriate, since Tiche-Goettinger's was the store that occupied the first two floors of the new Wilson Building.

There were many show windows in the building. Structuring

show windows was a new practice, because plate glass had not been accessible. The new thick glass was very expensive too. There were 80 feet of show windows on Main and Elm, and there were 200 feet of show windows on Ervay.

This building, the largest in Dallas in 1904, was truly a marvel. But the most remarkable accessory of all was the elevator. In fact, there were five of them. These elevators zipped people up to their doctors or dentists. The building was loaded with these profesionals. Those elevators took people up to their attorneys and CPAs. It was all very new and all very grand.

Mr. Wilson was definitely a family man, having five daughters, all of whom married very prominent Dallas businessmen. The baby girl, Geraldine, married Robert E. Lee Knight. The Knight family lived in the Oak Lawn area. Geraldine founded the Dallas Little Theatre which was on Maple Street. After her husband died she went on to star on Broadway. She took the stage name, Margaret Douglass, her grandmother's name. In New York, she starred in *Russet Mantle* by Lynn Riggs and *The Women* by Clare Booth Luce. Geraldine played the lead in the musical, *Bloomer Girl.* She portrayed Dolly Bloomer.

FIRST ELEVATOR #2

The Ambassador Hotel with its unique history claimed to have had the first passenger elevator in Dallas. The owners built the first Ambassador on the southwest corner of Jefferson and Crawford. It was called the Park Hotel. T. L. Marsalis had a large interest in the deal. The owners then built another hotel on Ervay Street in what was called The Cedars. This hotel was called the Majestic, and it was only a wooden building. Then in 1905, on the Ervay property the Ambassador Hotel as we know it today was built with an elevator to zip people right up to their rooms. C. H. Anderson was the architect.

This very classy hotel opened its doors to some very prominent visitors. John Phillip Sousa played a concert in City Park, so naturally for convenience he stayed at the Ambassador. President William Howard Taft, on a presidential visit to Dallas, also graced the premises of this hotel. When Sarah Bernhardt came to perform, she stayed at the Ambassador.

64

As the years went by, the Ambassador and the neighborhood around it deteriorated. It really became a pretty sleazy joint. Then later it was converted into a nursing home. Every time my mother went by the Ambassador, she always commented on how classy it had been. "I always wanted to stay at the Ambassador," she mused. When it became a nursing home, I threatened to put her in it. "Oh, I don't want to go there now."

Mother lived to see the hotel restored to its original grandeur. Unfortunately, due to the poor economy, it's in receivership now. Hopefully, someone can put it back into operation.

LAST ELEVATOR OPERATORS

When I was a kid, one was never alone on an elevator. There was a driver. The downtown Neiman Marcus store kept drivers for several years after the other department stores got automatic elevators. I think the managers thought this added to the mystique of the famous store. However, the last elevator driver in Dallas was on that extremely slow elevator, only going four stories, in the Old Red Courthouse. Finally, the county went modern and got an automatic elevator.

THE FIRST BAND IN DALLAS

Dallas had a band in 1872 led by Mr. John Hess. This gentleman came to Dallas in 1870 with the Swiss Colony that settled East of downtown. These Swiss people built their houses on a street which they appropriately named Swiss Avenue. The Meadows Foundation has restored a group of those old Victorian houses, and today, this charming area is known as the Wilson Block. These beautifully restored houses are offered to qualifying non-profit organizations to use for office space.

Nevertheless, Mr. Hess was a member of this first band and eventually became its leader. The instruments that this band used had been taken over by the city from a stranded road show. The traveling troop couldn't pay their bills after they finished their engagement, so the city took the only things of worth that belonged to the group as partial payment — their instruments. Having these instruments, the city then decided to organize a band in order to emphasize and encourage arts in Dallas.

Eventually, a teacher was engaged by the city to train and direct the volunteer musicians who showed up to play the confiscated instruments. The teacher pointed out that the instruments were actually worthless and that if Dallas really wanted a band, new horns would have to be forthcoming.

This music teacher floated a few loans using other people's money, of course. He sold subscriptions to the band season. He waged a very, very strenuous campaign and didn't stop until he had solicited $350. This money was triumphantly placed in the Jordon Bank, a trusted institution of the day, under the teacher's name. But alas, before the instruments were purchased, and before the band ever played publicly, the teacher disappeared and at the same time the money also "took wings." The quote is from the *Dallas News*.

Later, the teacher was found to be living in South America. He did not have the money any longer. Mr. John Hess had this to say. "We swore a few hackneyed oaths over our misfortune and went on with the old instruments, and soon we were playing well enough to meet all the requirements for engagements in saloons and beer halls." I just wonder if Meredith Willson read this story before he wrote, *The Music Man*.

THE FIRST LITTLE THEATRE PRODUCTION

The Little Theatre movement started in the United States in the 1920s and it was that year, 1920, that the first little theatre production was given in Dallas. Of course, there were school plays and traveling professionals and some stock companies, but the first time a group of folks got together and said, "Let's give a show!" was in December 1920. This action took place at the Unitarian Church, Emerson Hall, on South Ervay. H. Talbot Pearson, who was originally from Liverpool, England, who was here in Dallas dealing with his cotton export business, was the director. Later, he dropped cotton for the theatre. He became the first paid director of the Oak Cliff Little Theatre.

This first play was a French farce entitled, *A Scrap of Paper*. Seventy-five people came to see it. On that first night, there was a long wait between scenes, so one of the volunteer ticket sellers asked Elmer Scott to make a speech. "Quick, Elmer, we're losing our audience. Say something!" Elmer promptly replied, "What can I talk about?" The reply was immediate, "Talk about Dallas." He did!

WATER, WATER EVERYWHERE!

The Bachman's had a farm and a lake. In fact, Bachman Lake was really the only large body of water that God put in this area. The other lakes we now enjoy were created by civil engineers who were able to dig out land, dam off streams, and pray for rain. Voila — a lake! They are usually called reservoirs. The Dallas Parks and Recreation Department worked diligently in the 1920s with George Kessler, who truly had a grand plan for Dallas. Mayor W. J. Lawther, owner of a livestock feed manufacturing company, and prominent Park Board member, Emil Fretz, owner of a barber supply company, were behind Mr. Kessler all the way. These men were well aware of the lakes as water supply for the city. They were also interested in creating parks. This was good, because lakes make parks. George Kessler demanded extensive development of Bachman and White Rock Lakes, because these were to be water reservoirs that the city would eventually reach in a few years if all went as was predicted. As Dallas grew, the city couldn't stop with these lakes but had to go on. Lake Dallas was eventually used as the major water supply of the area. It was used until it dried up in the early 1950s. It was then that the city grew and the rains ceased. What a drought! I was at North Texas State University at that time, and we use to walk across the lake on dry ground. There was no water and Dallas suffered greatly from this. A person with a clean car or green grass was looked down upon. I remember my daddy saved his bath water for his favorite pecan tree.

Fort Worth did better with Lake Worth, so Dallas had to call on the neighboring town for some water. I don't wish to sound crude, but the truth was that the citizens of Dallas were drinking highly purified Fort Worth sewage. No one got sick, but everyone hated that water. I remember keeping Kool-Aid at the kitchen sink to flavor it. Signs popped up in restrooms all over Fort Worth. "Please flush. Dallas needs the water!" Yuk!

Well, don't worry. Dallas will never run out of water again. A new reservoir was developed in Grapevine in 1956, and another boost to the water supply came when Lake Ray Hubbard was developed in 1965.

Ray Hubbard, a Texas oil man, was the president of the Park Board from 1942 to 1971. Hubbard took the place of Robert G. Storey who was elected president of the Park Board in 1939. Storey

67

resigned in 1942 to enter the military service, and Hubbard went on the board serving until his death in 1971. Many, many of our marvelous parks were created when Ray Hubbard urged the city council to buy the land. They did. His long range planning made it possible for Dallas to have even more beautiful parks. Hubbard worked diligently with the Director of Parks, Louis B. Houston. Mr. Houston grew up on a farm between Prairie Dell and Salado, Texas. He thought he was going to Texas A&M, but when he heard that a student could go to school for six months at SMU and then work for six months, Houston came to Dallas and stayed.

After the Houston-Hubbard era there came another progressive time led by Grover Keeton, who started with the Dallas Parks Department in 1945. He served then as director of special activities and in 1972 was promoted to the top job. This is when my daughter, Jill, joined the Parks Department, so I have always had a very special interest in this part of our city government.

Well, parks and lakes abound in the city. Today, we have a brand new lake, Joe Pool. This lake was named for a gentleman who served in the Texas House of Representatives for three terms. Joe later ran for Congressman at large, won the race, and went to Washington. His untimely death at age 57 in 1968 was certainly a shock to his Texas supporters.

Nevertheless, God certainly supported the Joe Pool Lake project. After the dam was built, the rains came, and the lake was filled much sooner than expected.

RADIO

Dallas had the first municipally owned radio station west of the Mississippi. That station of 100 watts began broadcasting in 1921 with the call letters, WRR. Later the Federal Communications Commission announced that only stations east of the Mississippi would have call letters starting with a W. Those stations west of the river would have call letters starting with K. The early ones here kept the W — WFAA, WBAP, WRR.

The municipal station was started by a young electrical engineer, Henry Garrett, who worked for the fire department. His father was the beloved Episcopalian, Bishop Garrett. A park in east Dallas was named for this fine leader. His son, Henry, began to send out messages about fires to those trucks away from the fire stations. Later, between fire alarms, WRR played phonograph records for entertainment. Then news broadcasts were added. Eventually, news services got their own stations, and the municipal station was almost out of business. *Times Herald* owner Edwin J. Kiest raised funds to sustain WRR. And the station is still with us.

On November 9, 1947, a young navy lieutenant, Gordon McLendon, acquired permission from the FCC to begin broadcasting from a 1,000 watt station atop Cliff Towers, Oak Cliff. The call letters were appropriately chosen, KLIF.

During the war, Lt. McLendon broadcast in the Pacific at least three times a week, becoming the favorite voice of the guys on ships. In his satirical program, he rebroadcast Japanese progaganda with his own ad libs thrown in as the character, Lowell Gram Kaltenheatter. That name was derived from the names of WWII war correspondents. As that character, he took swipes at anything, including the brass, and the seamen loved him for it. His type of broadcast could not have been beamed to the mainland, but for the ships at sea, anything went.

Now, with the war over, McLendon, from his peaceful quarters at Cliff Towers, decided that his wartime character's ad libs would be great for returning servicemen and anyone else listening to KLIF. Dallas loved him — the old Scotsman, Gordon McLendon, as he billed himself. He was first to come up with "The top 40." He had flag pole sitters. There was a live blond on a billboard shelf waving to passing motorists. He taught a parrot to say KLIF by putting him in a room and bombarding the poor bird with call letters. The parrot started giving out the letters to get out of the room.

My kids grew up in the 50s and 60s with two great characters at KLIF — Irving Harrigan (Ron Chapman) and Charlie Brown (Jack Woods). These guys, like their boss, Gordon, took swipes at everyone including the brass.

Today KLIF-AM is successful with talk radio, Kevin McCarthy and Bob Ray Sanders. Ron Chapman, with his side-kick Susie Humphreys, is on KVIL-FM still taking swipes at everyone and everything.

CHAPTER V

Some Dallas Businesses

YOU COULD BANK ON IT

There's an old tale that the whittlers use to tell when they squatted for hours on the court house square, chewing, spitting, and yes, even whittling. The story was about a town where everyone was so honest, that the merchant was able to send his dog to the bank with the day's earnings. "Yep, I seen it! That dog was trained to pick up that money in his mouth and walk right up to the cashier's window and make the deposit!" Obviously, from that story we know that everyone in the town was honest including the dog. Well, at the turn of the century, the city of Dallas had that kind of honesty as well, because my mother as a small child was trained to take the day's earnings from her father's bakery (a bag of nickels and dimes), to walk down Main Street to the bank, and to make the deposit. No one ever bothered her. Of course, I do have to admit she was less a threat than the dog in the story, since Mother by nature wouldn't bite! Regardless, she was perfectly safe even though everyone knew she was carrying money. She'd make the deposit and amble back home. My mother loved doing this — her favorite chore. Banking as a child really made a lasting impression on my mother, because all of her life she always loved going to the bank!

Just a week before she died, I had to drive mother to the bank so she could make a deposit. She loved to do her own banking, she insisted that she always do it, and fortunately, she was able to do it until the day she died. I could never get her to move her account to a neighborhood bank. No!!! She had to go downtown to the First National Bank, because she had taken those nickels and dimes there as a child, so she was going to continue taking her nickels and dimes to the same bank. The bank had changed in size and locale, but to my mother it was always the same.

Actually, for years and years banking in Dallas never changed. In fact, it's just recently that the banking industry has made some shifts. There were name changes. First National is gone. It's now North Carolina National Bank of Texas (NCNB). There must be some of the old Dallas bankers rolling in their graves over some of those rather drastic changes.

FRED FLORENCE

Fred Florence, who was the President of Republic National Bank, pulled off one of the grandest Public Relations stunts in the history of the banking business. Beginning in the 1920s, every kid that enrolled in the Dallas schools automatically got an account with Republic National Bank. Every Tuesday, students brought their pennies, nickels, and dimes to school to put into their accounts. The homeroom teacher was the banker. This banking system went on throughout the "saving years." Today, if you told a kid to save his money, he wouldn't know what you were talking about.

Mr. Florence, himself, grew up a saver. In 1907, when he was seventeen years old, he got his first banking job — sorting checks and sweeping out the First National Bank, Rusk County. He saved his money for college and law school. However, when he was given the job of teller in that bank, he ran all the way home to tell his parents that he planned to be a banker, not a lawyer.

After serving in World War I, Fred Florence came to Dallas to work for the Guaranty Bank which later was called the Day and Night Bank. Still later, it merged with Republic National Bank, and today it's part of North Carolina National Bank of Texas.

71

Florence, the dynamic banker, had many friends, one of whom was the illustrious pastor of First Baptist Church, Dallas, Dr. W. A. Criswell. These two men frequented the same barber shop. In the 1940s, downtown business men loved to eavesdrop on and later tell about the conversations between Fred Florence and Dr. Criswell. In one chair sat the banker. In another chair sat the preacher. While the barbers snipped away, these two Dallas personalities would have fascinating and forceful tete-a-tetes. Needless to say, they grew closer as friends, so much so, that Dr. Criswell often pointed out that Fred Florence had "Baptist leanings." This was a bit unusual since Mr. Florence was Jewish and was married to Rabbi Daniel Lefkowitz's daughter.

"Really, Dr. Criswell," I said one day. "Fred Florence — a Baptist?????" Dr. Criswell was quick to reply. "Aaaah — in his heart — in his heart!" I would not argue that point. Only God knows.

Speaking of God, banking, and Dr. Criswell, I remember my days of teaching Vacation Bible School. I always requested to teach the third grade. Third graders are so sincere and so honest. These traits lead to a lot of fun. When Dr. Criswell visited the Vacation Bible School, he asked the kids if they were planning to go on a vacation. "Oh, sure, we're going to Disneyland," came the response. "Fine," Dr. Criswell cheered. "Now, what is the first thing you put into your suitcase when you go?" Dr. Criswell had been going places for years and the first thing he put into his suitcase was the Bible. He waited for the proper response — the Bible. He forgot that these kids live in a different world, so the answer was quite startling. "Yes, little one. What is the first thing you put into your suitcase when you go?" The answer boomed from the tiny body, "Credit cards!" Dr. Criswell was speechless and Fred Florence rolled over in his grave.

ROBERT L. THORNTON

Robert L. Thornton was born August 10, 1880, Hamilton, Texas. His family eventually moved to Ellis County where Bob picked cotton for a living. He prided himself in that he could pick 500 pounds of cotton a day. In 1904, he came to Dallas and got a room in a boarding house, 219 Ross Avenue, Mrs. S. L. Johnson,

72

proprietor. This was when he decided to become a candy salesman. Finally, he had enough money saved to go into business with a partner, Metta Stiles. They opened a book store. Bob Thornton owned a book store, but he had never read a book. This was the first time in history that this had happened. He lost money on the book store, but he certainly did not lose on the next business. At the age of thirty-six, he opened a bank west of Lamar Street, 704 Main Street — the Stiles, Thornton and Lund Bank. This bank specialized in automobile loans and was very profitable. It was later called the Mercantile Bank — now Bank One.

Bob Thornton built a tall building with four clocks on it — the Mercantile Bank Building — now so overshadowed by the newer skyscrapers. My daddy had his office in this building and often saw Uncle Bob in the elevator. One day, Mr. Thornton was approached in the elevator by an eager symphony fan. "Mr. Thornton, would you give to the Dallas Symphony Orchestra?" The reply came immediately. "Sure would. Just don't make me go to the concerts. I only like music that I can pat my foot to."

When R. L. Thornton was Mayor of Dallas, he saw to it that the City Council meetings were brisk and business like. "If it's a DO meeting, I'm available. If it's a DON'T meeting, I ain't interested." He was a doer. Thornton saw to it that a woman was on the city council — first one — Mrs. Carr P. Collins, Jr. He pointed out that a city was like a man. "If a man don't have anything to do, he gets restless and accomplishes less, for himself and everybody else. As long as a city is moving and doing — keeping busy — that city is going to continue to grow. Let's keep the dirt flyin'."

W. H. GASTON

Dr. Robert W. Glover, head of the History Department at Tyler Junior College, found in an abandoned log cabin in the East Texas piney woods a series of letters written by two boys, Robert and William Gaston. These letters described in detail the Battle of Richmond, 1862. Obviously, the parents of the boys had lived in the cabin and the mother had hidden the cherished letters. Fortunately, Dr. Glover found them and published them in a book, *Tyler to Sharpsburg*. He included in the book, the story of the Gastons. He tells of how W. H. Gaston finally got to Dallas after the Civil

73

War and of how he eventually founded Republic National Bank. William's brother, Robert, never returned. He lost his life in the Battle of Richmond. Actually, most of the letters were written by Robert Gaston, but after he was killed, the surviving brother, William, took up the correspondence.

The Gaston story begins with Colonel and Mrs. R. K. Gaston, members of a well known South Carolina family. Their sons, Robert and William, were born in Wilcox County, Alabama. In 1849, like so many Southerners, the Gastons came to Texas and settled in Anderson County, East Texas. Later they came to live in Smith County where the Colonel was elected to serve in the Texas Legislature.

When the war came in 1861, the boys enlisted in the Texas Guards, organized in Palestine, Texas, by Captain A. T. Rainey. The Guards made their way to Richmond where they became part of General John B. Hood's famous Brigade.

William was elected Captain and was called Boy Captain of Hood's Brigade. The tough Texans became well known for their bravery and their reckless attitude in battle at Manasas, Sharpsburg and Fredericksburg.

Unfortunately, Robert Gaston was killed at Richmond in June 1862, and William applied for and received a transfer to the Trans-Mississippi Department. For the remainder of the war, he was stationed at Galveston. There he served as the aide-de-camp to his former regimental commander, A. T. Rainey, who had been seriously wounded at Gaines' Mill.

After the war W. H. Gaston returned to Anderson County where he married Miss Laura Furlow. She lived only a few years. William then married her sister, Miss Ion Furlow and with her reared a family, three sons and two daughters.

Eventually, W. H. Gaston moved to Dallas with his family. Here he prospered and eventually became President of Gaston National Bank. Later this bank became Republic National Bank. He developed the street railway system and he gave the land for the State Fair grounds to name a couple of his civic contributions. W. H. Gaston lived to be 87 years old.

Here's an excerpt from a letter written from Richmond, June 29, 1862.

Had daylight lasted two hours longer we would have ruined

the right wing of the grand army. We slept on the battlefield within 300 yards of the Yankee lines. A person might think that it would be a horrible thing to sleep on the battlefield, and so it is. But we were so worn out that we could have slept anywhere. When we went into the fight we laid aside our blankets and knapsacks on the field and we soon supplied ourselves with enough of these to sleep comfortable. Every time we woke up we could hear the shrieks of the wounded and dying, some calling for their regiments, others for their friends and relatives. This seems truly horrible now, but at the time would excite very little emotion. The wounded Yankees would appear very thankful when ever we would give them water or any assistance. A great many of them said that they had been taught by their Generals to expect no such favors at our hands, that we would murder them without mercy if they fell into our hands.

When morning came the enemy had retreated back several miles and were nearly all across the Chickahominy. Directly after daylight we saw a white flag coming slowly through the woods in front of our regiment from the direction of the enemy. Our pickets halted it and Gen. Hood went to see to it, when a Colonel, Captain and 3 privates surrendered to him. They said they had lost their regiment and were tired down hunting it. Every prisoner we took seemed very well satisfied. When they would pass us, our boys would hollow "On to Richmond." The Yankees would frequently reply that they knew they could get there one way or the other.

While resupplying ourselves with ammunition, Gen. Wingfall made us a speech in which he complemented us in the highest terms. Gen. Hood also made us a little speech, though he is a better soldier than speaker.

If I had time I could write you many interesting things but I have neither time nor paper. Love. Your affectionate son. W. H. Gaston.

NATHAN ADAMS

Nathan Adams was born November 26, 1869, in Giles County, Tennessee. His father died when he was five years old, so his mother was forced to become the support of the family. She taught school, and since teaching school did not bring in too much money, little Nathan was reared in near poverty. Somehow, he managed to finish school and go on to Giles County College. His college career was cut short, however, because again there just wasn't enough money to keep going. He began to work at the Giles County Bank for the grand salary of $8.33 a month. An attorney for the Texas and Pacific Railroad was in Giles County trying to obtain some records for a case he was handling. The railroad was being sued, and this attorney, John Wilkes, needed some banking records. Young Nathan Adams secured the records for the attorney in perfect form. The lawyer was impressed. In fact, Mr. Wilkes was so impressed, he offered the young man a job with the railroad in Dallas. Nathan Adams decided that going to Dallas was the thing to do. He arrived in Dallas, Texas, December 28, 1887, with $4 in his pocket. Adams immediately checked into the St. George Hotel and reported to the railroad for his job, January 1, 1888. He carried this note, "Here's the young man I was telling you about."

Nathan Adams was with the railroad only a few months, and then he felt that he was better off in banking. He got a job with the National Exchange Bank. Here, Nathan served as a teller, then as a cashier, then as an advisor, and up, up, up, up the ladder in the banking business, until he was the president of First National Bank of Dallas. He brought about the merger of the American Exchange National Bank with City National Bank to make First National Bank. Nathan Adams served as President until he retired in 1949 at the age of 80 years.

This man was a tremendous leader and a giver of love. He had a great part in the founding of the Scottish Rite Hospital for Crippled Children. Often he went to the hospital to read to the children. He was also a big supporter of the Dallas Eagles, the baseball team. Nathan Adams led in the contributions to the Community Chest, forerunner of the United Fund. During World War II, he worked in the War Lone Drive and received a tribute from Henry Morgenthau, Secretary of the Treasury.

When Nathan Adams retired from the presidency of First National Bank, he was asked the secret of his longevity. "I never worry. I leave that bank down on Main Street. I give my time to lots of interests." He also pointed out that young people always wanted to start at the top. This he said, was impossible.

There was a big recognition dinner when he retired. Dechard Anderson Hulcy, president of the Chamber of Commerce, said, "God has blessed the great city of Dallas with Nathan Adams."

When Nathan Adams was ninety-three years old he became very ill and moved into the very hospital he founded, Scottish Rite Hospital. He lived there for four years until he died at ninety-seven. The *Morning News* presented a story of his life. They called it a *Salute to an Old Red Fez*.

ROBERT L. THORNTON AND THE FAIR PARK

National historical recognition has been given to the Fair Park, Dallas, Texas. It is the largest display of *art deco* in the country. Going out to the Fair Park is like stepping into a 1930s time capsule. The buildings were constructed, the grounds were beautified, the atmosphere was set for the 1936 Texas Centennial. Texas was one hundred years old, 1836–1936.

The grandest building of all at the Fair Park is the Hall of State. This elegant structure was built for 1.2 million dollars. At the Centennial celebration, 24 search lights pierced the night sky and set out a thrilling invitation to all that could see them. Come, come to the party!

Thousands of people did come. President Roosevelt came with the beloved Eleanor. The presidential motorcade entered the Cotton Bowl, which was also built at that time, and FDR was driven up to the platform. There he addressed the nation on radio. Also on that platform stood Robert L. Thornton, the man responsible for the whole thing.

We Dallasites all owe Uncle Bob a big "Thank You" because he did bring the Centennial to Dallas. The planning of this 100th anniversary started in Corsicana, Texas, 1923. It was then a group got together to plan this great event that would happen in 1936.

The group wanted plenty of time to get ready. After all, the Chicago World's Fair, the Columbian Exhibition, honoring the 400th year of the discovery of America by Christopher Columbus, was a year late. The fair should have been in 1892. but the fair was held in 1893. The committee didn't get it together in time.

The St. Louis World's Fair was also a year late. The Louisiana Purchase was made in 1803. The fair in St. Louis was in 1904. This committee, too, was a year late.

Texas wanted their big moment celebrated on time, so they started early. Unfortunately, the planning committee appointed a man who couldn't get the thing off the ground. Jesse Holman Jones of Houston, financier, builder, publisher, and philanthropist, seemed to be the perfect man for the job. However, he fizzled early, and the Centennial almost didn't come to pass.

The Governor of Texas in 1923 was Pat Neff, who was very much in favor of the Centennial committee. This was good, because Neff was to get some state money for the project. However, with Jones at the head, the whole project stayed in trouble. He hesitated and he procrastinated. The fair became a dream that no one thought would materialize.

Still there were those who stated loudly and clearly, "We want a Centennial that will attract the entire world to our gates."

Delegates from Houston just knew that the world would come to Houston for the big celebration. After all, Sam Houston bled all over Harris County in the battle of San Jacinto. Houston was the port city — the biggest city in Texas. The Centennial must be in Houston!

Delegates from San Antonio never gave the situation a second thought. The Centennial must be in San Antonio. After all, the Alamo was there — the Shrine of Texas Liberty. The whole affair would be built around the Alamo.

Those on the committee from Austin thought that the big shindig must be in Austin, the State Capitol. The Governor could step out on the porch of his mansion and wave to the crowds.

Amon Carter, Mayor of Fort Worth, never got involved. He planned his own party and never left his beloved city. He didn't care if anyone came to Fort Worth or not!

R. L. Thornton, Mayor of Dallas, arrived. Thornton had locked up the rich men of the city and had not let them out until he had some money — lots of money! He sewed up the Centennial deal when he said, "We have no history, but here's 10 million dollars — cash! The party's in Dallas!"

It was obvious that Houston's urban bureaucracy lacked leadership and direction, so they didn't get the celebration. San Antonio and Austin had the same problem. They thought they could get by on their historical past. R. L. Thornton knew that money talked, especially during the depression. He also was a man of action. Forty years later, John Stemmons paid Thornton a high tribute. "The genius of this town, Dallas, has been good government, good clean honest government. The Thornton Era provided the city with this unsurpassed quality."

When the money was plunked down at the meeting, someone asked, "Bob, every fair needs an esplanade. Does Dallas have an esplanade?" Thornton replied, "We have two!" Then he turned to a friend and asked, "What in the heck is an esplanade?"

Well, if you go to the Fair, you'll see in the front of the Hall of State a statue of Bob Thornton in bronze, hat in hand, and he's looking out over his esplanade!

MAYOR CHARLES TURNER

In 1932, Charles Turner was elected mayor of the city of Dallas. 1932 — the year I was born! He was born in Richardson, Texas, in 1885. His family eventually moved to Oak Cliff where he grew up. As a young man, he worked as a drug salesman — legitimate!!! His career was interrupted by World War I. In no time at all, he was off to France in the AEF. When he was discharged, he held the rank of Captain.

Turner returned to his business and like everything in the country it boomed until that fateful day in October 1929. The market crashed. The depression set in! Charles Turner was the depression mayor who was able to get federal funds to keep the soup kitchens open for those who were hungry. He also worked with R. L. Thornton on the Centennial celebration. Turner's "baby" was the Cavalcade of Texas, the pageant written by Jan Isbelle Fortune that was presented every evening during the celebration. Unfortunately, Mayor Turner died before the big extravaganza opened. The city grieved over the loss of this dear friend. The Cavalcade of Texas opened on schedule, and the show was dedicated to Mayor Charles Turner.

THE BATTLE OF THE SHOWS, THE BATTLE OF THE CITIES

In the last scene of the movie, *Funny Girl*, Billy Rose, played by James Caan, turns to Fannie Brice, played by Barbra Streisand, and says, "I'm going to Fort Worth, Texas, to build a theatre for Amon Carter. It will be called Casa Manana." And so it was! This "House of Tomorrow" was built for Amon Carter by Billy Rose in

Fort Worth, and this Casa Manana of 1936, gave the Texas Centennial in Dallas some real stiff competition.

Three days before Dallas celebrated its millionth visitor, July 18, 1936, the Frontier Centennial in Fort Worth opened. Amon Carter was still looking for federal money to keep his whole operation solvent. Eventually, General Motors came through with a very appreciated $22,000, a fortune in 1936. Billy Rose ran as fast as he could to his office on the centennial grounds. He wrote the contract with GM on the back of a piece of music. The big automotive company saved Casa Manana.

Even though there was a money shortage, the performers were rehearsing. The shows in Fort Worth were going on. A twenty-four piece band was rehearsing for the show *Jumbo* in a room in the Medical Arts Building. Paul Whiteman's orchestra was in a hotel ballroom. The dancers were hopping around in Monnig's warehouse. At the Last Frontier arena, several numbers were being staged. Those rehearsals were gruelling and strenuous, but after all, it was depression time, and suddenly show people were working and 102 musicians were playing, so no one complained. The weekly pay ran about $55. Some of the featured performers got a little more.

Billy Rose did it! Amon Carter did it! The world's largest outdoor theatre-restaurant was gong to open. As Cater said, "We'll show those Eastern dudes. They'll learn about Broadway on the prairie." Carter also wanted to show the citizens of Dallas what Fort Worth could do. He dared to raise a very controversial sign right across the street from the Texas Centennial in Dallas, saying, "Come to Fort Worth — Billy Rose, Paul Whiteman and Sally Rand are there. Only 45 minutes away." This sign lighted up the whole of Parry Street directly across from the grand entrance of the Texas Centennial.

Sally Rand was a stripper who stripped and then artistically covered her curvaceous body with hugh fans. She came to Fort Worth with girls from her NUDE Ranch!!!!

Amon Carter made a deal with the Liquor Control Board. Officers agreed to go blind while Fort Worth celebrated. The press began to describe Dallas as the "great lemon and strawberry pop fair," and attendance at the Dallas party did begin to drop off. R. L. Thornton set to work immediately. "We're going to open up this town!" Thornton made *his* arrangements with the Liquor Control Board.

The shows in Fort Worth were bringing in record-breaking crowds. Meanwhile in Dallas, on July 20, 1936, a violent thunderstorm swept the exposition causing $23,000 in damages. Lightning struck the Cavalcade Show and damaged the scenery. The temperature rose. The rain was to bring some cooling relief, but instead the temperature reached 105 degrees. Of course, the heat affected the outdoor performances in Fort Worth, but at that point it looked like Fort Worth was winning the audiences.

Dallas was desperate now. How could more people be brought to the fair? Cities across the state were given "their days." Example — San Marcos Day! A special train would carry a mob from San Marcos for $4.81, round trip. The Southwest Texas State Teachers College band was invited to play. This "city" plan did bring in some additional people.

Dallas declared a special celebrity day and hauled in Robert Taylor, Allan Jones, Bob Burns, and Ginger Rogers. Amon Carter wished for his buddy, Will Rogers.

It was the battle of the shows. It was the battle of the cities. Actually, Dallas and Fort Worth waged war for years after the 1936 Centennial was long over. In fact, the first thing that the cities ever did together was to build the Dallas-Fort Worth International Airport.

Well, those shows ended over 50 years ago. On Saturday, November 14, 1936, the last performance was scheduled for *Jumbo* and the show at the Frontier Palace also ended. The song that Billy Rose wrote for Casa Manana, "The Night is Young and You're so Beautiful," was sung for the last time that evening. Rose turned to Carter and said, "I build shows. You build cities."

Today, a new Casa Manana, built in 1958, stands on the corner of University and Camp Bowie. Crumbling parts of the old Pioneer Palace stood next to the new theatre as late as 1968.

After 7 million people came to the Texas Centennial in Dallas, it closed in early November. At Studio B. Gulf Studios, the final broadcast was aired. The lights on the Esplanade were turned off. One person made this statement about the fair grounds and the buildings: "A jilted lover stands alone in South Dallas, shivering under the belated touch of winter, and wonders where her admirers have gone."

Well, the Fair Grounds in Dallas light up every year in October for the biggest state fair in the nation. Of course, there are other activities going on there all year long. And Casa Manana, in its new home, is open all year. There is a children's theatre that offers very professional productions and in the summer, Broadway shows are on the marquee. My husband, Jack, has been the Casa drummer and percussionist since 1960. He's been in that orchestra pit for over thirty years, and he's mighty proud of it. I have appeared on stage at Casa many times in various roles, and I love every minute that I'm there. I can feel the spirits of Billy Rose and Amon Carter every time I step upon that stage.

THE JITNEY

My mother often spoke of taking a jitney. The dictionary explains that a jitney is a motor vehicle that carries passengers for a small fare. This definition isn't quite right. It should be stated in the past tense — *carried* people — because regulations in the transportation business brought an end to the jitney. Later, the word, jitney, became a slang term meaning five cents, because five cents was the usual charge for a ride.

In 1915, there was no transportation to Cement City, Gates, Sowers, Irving, and other points west. Seeing this as a problem, Mr. V. G. Schrader acquired two Model T Fords which he used for a jitney route that started two blocks from the court house on Record Street at Commerce where Mr. Skillern had his drug store. It went west on Commerce to Beckley, turned north on Beckley to Singleton, and then turned west on Singleton to various stops west. Since there were only two cars and quite a few people who needed transportation, it was not unusual at peak hours to see people hanging from the running boards as the feisty Ford putt-putted across the viaduct on its way west. During the slack hours the jitney would take people to funerals and hospitals.

V. C. Bilbo, fondly called "Red," drove the Schrader jitney. He loved to tell the story of meeting another car on a narrow dirt road head on, and of the drivers fighting it out as to which one would move over so the other could pass. Bilbo's customers urged him on in the fight. The passengers from the other car, of course, rooted for their driver. A free-for-all broke out and a good time was had by all.

Eventually, Mr. Schrader sold out to Bilbo. Actually, there were only two cars involved in the deal, so it wasn't a big sell out. However, Bilbo, being a good businessman, soon acquired five cars. He was able to pack 30 people into those five cars. Passengers rode knee to knee, or some sat on other passengers' laps.

Again, at peak hours people were on the running boards and fenders. Everyone managed to hang on, even though the roads were rough and bumpy. When it rained, Bilbo and his drivers would take people to their doorsteps. Obviously, he was loved by the working girls and the elderly, who always needed a little special care. It was a fact that funerals were often scheduled to accommodate the jitney schedule.

Mr. Bilbo also took the kids to school events — declamation contests, spelling bees, football games, etc. Sometimes, he would deliver groceries and prescriptions.

In 1927, the Texas legislature enfranchised the bus service. Bus companies and railroads had to have permits to function. There were too many regulations for Mr. Bilbo's jitney, so the line was discontinued and the last running board ride was taken.

Victor Clifford Bilbo was born near Hillsboro, June 8, 1894. He left home at age ten to seek his fortune. He was a friendly person who claimed that he could even make friends with the Indians who were still around. Never afraid of hard work, he became a mule skinner for the company that built the railroad through Sherman and Denison. Arriving in Dallas in 1910, he went to work for Lewe's Sand and Gravel Company. He finally bought his own mules and wagons and hauled gravel for Mr. Stemmons when he was developing part of Oak Cliff. After watching people drive cars, Bilbo decided that he too could drive, and that's when he began to drive for Mr. Schrader.

In 1927, when his jitney line came to an end, Bilbo went into the trucking business. In the meantime, he was a car salesman selling Fords for the whopping price of $160. He owned and operated a garage and gas pump station near the court house. Eventually he went into heavy hauling of oil field equipment and livestock. A&P Supermarkets were also his customers. Eventually, Mr. Bilbo owned a chicken ranch in Irving and two cattle ranches in Hamilton and Fort Worth. He retired in 1955 and died in 1968. He is buried in Laurel Land Cemetery.

SANGER BROTHERS — GOOD SCOUTS

Isaac Sanger came to America from Bavaria and arrived in Texas in 1857. His younger brothers, Lehman and Philip, arrived just in time to join him in the Confederate Army. After the Civil War, the brothers opened stores in many little Texas towns. Wherever the railroad went, so did the brothers. There were stores in Bryan, Hearne, Calvert, Bremond, Groesbeck — just to name a few. They stocked goods that Texans needed at that time — everything from Bowie knives to musical instruments. Eventually, they saw a real future in Dallas, a city they felt was destined to grow. The Sanger Brothers had a little frame store on Elm Street. They lived in one room behind that store. They prospered here, so eventually they were able to buy the land on Main Street behind the Elm Street Store. Finally, they had the whole block and later built a six story building on Elm, Main, and Lamar. Still much later, Sanger Brothers moved to Akard and Pacific. They also opened stores at all the shopping malls. The Lamar Street store was sold to Dallas County, and El Centro College occupies the six story building on Elm, Main, and Lamar.

As a kid, I loved to go into the old Sanger Brothers, because on the first floor they featured the Girl Scout Shop. I bought my uniform, mess kit, hand book — everything I needed as a scout. The Girl Scout Headquarters, established in Dallas in 1924, was out at the Fair Park in the Little Scout House. Here was where the scout leaders went to buy the pins, badges, etc. — the official stuff. We girls hung out at Sanger Brothers.

Everything has changed. Sanger Brothers is now Foleys. The Scout headquarters is out on Skillman Avenue in a beautiful new building.

NEIMAN MARCUS

Our famous Dallas storekeeper, Stanley Marcus, inherited the fabulous store, Neiman Marcus, from his father, Herbert. Herbert Marcus was offered the Coca-Cola franchise but decided that the drink would never sell, so he became a millionaire in the dry goods business. His son, Stanley, when he took over the store was prompt in making the store even more fabulous than it was. There is a mystique about Neiman Marcus and there will always be. An aura hangs over the luxurious store.

When I graduated from high school, I wanted all of my senior clothes to come from Neimans. I remember announcing, "I must have Neiman Marcus clothes or I will not graduate!" Mother must have taken me seriously, because my senior day, baccalaureate, and graduation dresses all came from Neiman Marcus. Then when I went off to college, that special suit was also purchased at Neimans.

I have a dear friend who is a lab technician. Now, lab technicians deal with specimens in jars. One day, a lady decided to liven up the lab. She had her specimen brought over in a Neiman Marcus jar, in a Neiman Marcus shopping bag, delivered by a Neiman Marcus truck. Needless to say, it brightened the day. The fun — the game — the joke — would never have worked with any store other than Neiman Marcus.

One summer, my son, Phil, when he was in high school, worked as a delivery boy for Neiman Marcus. We waited each evening for him to come home to tell us all about the exotic things that he had delivered. He toted everything from French toilets to French tutus. That was a great "learning" summer for my son. As a delivery boy, when he rang the doorbell, he was immediately ordered by the maid of the house to go to the back door. My son had been a front door kid all of his life. It was great for him to learn a little humbleness. He soon discovered that delivery boys go to the back door even if they are from Neiman Marcus.

TITCHE GOETTINGERS

My mother went to school with Cordelia Titche. Her father owned and operated Titche Goettingers, a department store that occupied the Wilson Building on the northwest corner of Main and Ervay. Later, the store moved into a new building constructed on the corner of Elm and St. Paul. This building stands empty today — a sad sight for someone who remembers so well the great days of Titche-Goettingers.

First and foremost, I remember in Titches the perfume fountain that was prominently displayed and running on the first floor by the Elm Street entrance. No lady in the 1930s or 1940s ever put perfume on at home. They all waited to douse themselves at the perfume fountain in Titches. It took over two gallons of perfume a week to keep the fountain running. There were the "dippers" who took way more than a splash when they went by the sweet smelling spring. Then, of course, evaporation counted for some of the loss. Nevertheless, that perfume fountain at Titches was an important feature of downtown Dallas.

Then there was the auditorium on the seventh floor. Here is where Evelyn Oppenheimer and Mrs. Emery reviewed books for the ladies on certain mornings each week. The oral book review was an important social event that brought ladies into the store. Some of these patrons would buy a book, or they would certainly buy something, and any sale during the depression was important.

At Christmas time the seventh floor was turned into Santa's workshop and all of the kids went up there to see the latest toy to come out of the North Pole. Santa himself was on hand so all the Christmas wishes could be told to him.

Some dancing, piano, and expression teachers used the auditorium as a recital hall for their students. I gave many readings, tapped many dances, and played many piano pieces in that auditorium.

On the second floor, there was the tea room which featured style shows on certain days. At that time, department stores imported impressive dressmakers to be "in residence." These prima dommas took themselves quite seriously. A woman who was into fashion also took them seriously. These dressmakers were always addressed as Madame. Tiche-Goettingers had Madame Snow who designed special attire for the fashion conscious society matrons of Dallas. A Madame Snow creation was a must for the woman who attended the various balls and concerts held for Dallas society.

Personally, I loved Titches' basement. A customer could enter the front door, turn right, and go down the stairs to take in the greatest sales. Also the large restrooms were in the basement. And that's what they were — restrooms. Large comfortable couches accommodated ladies who had to rest from shopping and who had to take a puff or two on a cigarette. Women in the 1930s never smoked in public, and I remember as a kid I loved to go into Titches' restroom and watch women smoke. In fact, I expressed these feelings aloud once. "Come, dear," Mother said. "Oh, please, Mother. Can't we stay a little longer. I just love to watch these women

smoke." Mother jerked me out amid a lot of laughter from understanding women smokers.

When Northpark, the first shopping mall opened in Dallas,
Titches was a major store at the mall. In the 70s, Joskes took over,
and now Dillard's has its name upon the old Tiche-Goettinger
Stores. We, with long memories, will always love Titches.

PEGASUS AND MOBIL OIL

"It's a great peg driven into the ground holding Dallas in its
place from no matter which direction the town is approached." This
statement was made by a very enthusiastic journalist as he looked at
the Magnolia Oil Building, when it opened, August 14, 1922, corner of Commerce and Akard. For us natives the Magnolia Oil
Building of 29 stories was the grandest and most imposing edifice in
the Southwest. It made Dallas a city.

The Magnolia Petroleum Company was the producer of So-
cony and later, Mobil Petroleum products. Magnolia was a pio-
neering force in the oil industry starting as a series of smaller companies. Actually, it rose from the Spindletop find near Beaumont,
one of the greatest oil discoveries ever made.

That oil was discovered when Patillo Higgins, a super tough
guy from Beaumont who suddenly got religion, took his Baptist
Sunday school class out on a picnic near some springs on a hill called
Spindletop. The rainbow colors in the water and the smell of that
water convinced Higgins that there was oil. He finally got enough
money together to drill and on January 10, 1901, the big 'un came
in and the world has never been the same. Dallas certainly wasn't the
same, especially when Magnolia decided to make the city its corporate headquarters.

Sir Alred Charles Bossom, internationally known architect,
author, critic, and statesman, born in 1881, a Baron in the British
nobility, designed the building. He was trained at the St. Thomas
School and the Architectural School of the Royal Academy of the
Arts. He established offices in New York in 1903 and in the years
to follow became very well known throughout the world as a builder
of grand buildings. His Dallas structure of Renaissance design cost
4 million dollars to build in the early 1920s. Every office has an
outside view built by the design following the "court construction"

method. There are Italian marble floors and American walnut woodwork. There are 500 offices and 16 elevators. The whole point of the building was to establish Dallas as an oil capital and the building certainly did this.

Then the icing on the cake came twelve years later, November 8, 1934. Pegasus, the flying red horse, the symbol for Magnolia Oil, was placed on top. Whenever I take anyone on tour of Dallas, I always point out that there are actually two horses up there. Having two horses gave Dallas the distinction of no longer being "a one horse town." Actually, it was necessary to have two horses so that the wind wouldn't blow the beloved figure down.

In 1934, the American Petroleum Institute Convention was held in Dallas. Magnolia Oil went to Tex Lite, a company that made signs, and ordered a sign for the top of the Magnolia Building. Their logo had to rotate and also had to be seen all over Dallas. Magnolia placed the order in September and wanted it by November 8. This gigantic and almost impossible project was given to the treasurer and chief engineer of the company, Mr. J. B. McMath. Mr. McMath was not a schooled engineer, he was just smart. He had come to Dallas in 1917 and had done well with his mechanical abilities. Now, he really had an almost unthinkable undertaking. Right off, Mr. McMath knew that there had to be two horses with the mechanics stationed between them. The horses were made, 30 by 40 feet. Now, how was he going to make the monster turn? One evening J. B. McMath went to sleep, and in a dream the whole mechanical precept was given to him. He always claimed that God laid out the plans in that dream. In fact, this gentleman always gave God the credit for any of his accomplishments. Therefore, a giant wheel was made that would run on a circular track that could be electrically powered to make that horse go round and round. It worked!

The parts of big Pegasus were taken up on the elevators of the building, and finally the horse was in place. All was ready but the lighting. The neon tubing was not on. Unfortunately, just when the tubing was ready to be placed, Tex Lite burned to the ground, so the tubing had to be reblown right up on top of the building itself. By November 7, 1934, the whole project was completed and on November 8, 1934, the magnificent flying red horse was turned on. It rotated and it was seen all over Dallas. That horse turned until the 1970s when the electricity was shut off. Just a little power and Pegasus would start revolving again.

As a child I remember I could see that horse from my backyard only if my daddy would lift me up on his shoulders. This was a great thrill. On summer nights, I wouldn't go to bed until Daddy had boosted me up so that I could tell the Magnolia horse good night. Kind of corny — but true. We Dallas natives love Pegasus!

7 ELEVEN

Southland Corporation was founded in Dallas. Recently, the company declared bankruptcy, but with some Japanese money, the corporation was saved. 7 Eleven will go on. The stores will continue to stay open all over the world, offering the infamous Slurpees.

Actually, the 7 Eleven saga starts with an Oxford graduate, Samuel Insull, who left England in 1881 to work with Thomas Edison and his electrical company. Mr. Insull traveled all over the country promoting the Edison Company and the Commonwealth Electric Company. This company was bringing electricity and with this new power, something called refrigeration. Ice companies realized that there was going to be a change. It was obvious that the faithful old ice man was going to be a thing of the past. People would be able to get refrigeration in their homes and ice houses were going to have to offer much more than just ice.

There were some fine business men who offered the citizens of Dallas their supply of ice — Claude S. Dawley, J. O. Jones, and Uncle Johnny Green. But it was an Oak Cliff High School graduate, Joe C. Thompson Jr., that offered business men who were selling ice, a new merchandising plan. Thompson created the world's first convenience store on the corner of Twelfth and Edgefield, Dallas, Texas. He called it the Tote'm Store. This happened in the summer of 1927. By 1939, there were 60 of these retail stores. After World War II, the stores boasted that they were open from 7 A.M. until 11 P.M. Tracy-Locke Advertising Agency came up with a new name, 7 Eleven.

In 1971, 7 Eleven, Southland Corporation, made its initial entry into the European market through the purchase of 370 specialty shops of Cavenham Limited, a large manufacturer, distributor, exporter and wholesaler of grocery, bakery, liquor, tobacco, candy and pharmaceutical products in England and Scotland. Later, in 1972, Southland acquired controlling interests in Wright's Biscuits Ltd. and Moore's Stores Ltd., which operated 840 retail grocery outlets in England, Scotland and Wales.

Now, the Japanese market is opening even wider for the company. As the slogan goes, "Oh, thank heaven for 7 Eleven."

HEALTH INSURANCE BEGAN IN DALLAS, BLUE CROSS, BLUE SHIELD

Dr. Justin Ford Kimball was Superintendent of the Dallas schools beginning in 1914. He got into the business world in a very unique way — helping his teachers. In those days, teachers made the lowest salaries of any professional group. Actually, they still do. Nevertheless, the teachers were so poor that when they got sick, they just had to die. They couldn't afford to go to the hospital or get proper medical care. Poor things! This bothered Dr. Kimball, so the thought came to him. Why not set a little money aside for the day that illness may come? He took 25¢ from each teacher each month, put this money in a fund at Baylor Hospital, and created what was called the Baylor Plan. When a teacher had to go to the hospital, the money was there at Baylor. No one had ever thought of prepaid hospitalization before. This plan eventually became known as Blue Cross, Blue Shield. It all started in Dallas.

Dr. Kimball was offered a percentage of each policy sold, but he refused to make money on his beloved teachers. The *Dallas Morning News* employees were the next to take on the Blue Cross Plan. Here again, Dr. Kimball could have demanded his cut, but he never did. He remained the humble but powerful man that he always was.

When I was a kid, I took piano lessons with and appeared on piano recitals with Nancy Kimball. She was just a kid like all of us, except we did know that her father was fairly well known. Nancy today is a nurse in Austin, Texas. She admits that her daddy could have been a millionaire several times over, but he didn't choose to take the money.

THE DIME STORE

A store clerk in Watertown, New York, Frank Winfield Woolworth, 27 years of age, persuaded his employer to install a counter on which all goods were priced at 5 cents. The idea proved

90

to be successful. Woolworth then induced a man to lend him $400 to open a five cent store in Utica, New York. This store failed in three months. Woolworth then persuaded the same man to try another store, this time in Lancaster, Pennsylvania. This store would feature 5 cent and 10 cent wares. This store made money. In fact, this store made so much money that Woolworth opened stores in Philadelphia, Erie, Newark, Scranton, New York City, and Buffalo. By 1913, with nickels and dimes, Woolworth built the tallest building in the world — The Cathedral of Commerce — 60 stories tall.

When I was a kid, the dime store was the best baby sitter in the world. Give a kid a dime and a dime store, and that kid was occupied for at least three hours. Today, a dime buys nothing, so the dime store is almost a thing of the past. Woolworth still has three stores in Dallas — Northpark, Preston Center, and Big Town. They're seemingly doing well. And too, there is another company that still holds on to the old dime store philosophy, a company that was born in Texas, a company that is doing quite well — M. E. Moses.

When my son, Phil, was a little boy, he had trouble saving his money. I knew that my mother had given him a couple of dollars, and I knew that this money was burning a hole in his pocket. Surely enough, he came to me and begged. "Could we go to Ben Franklin (Dime Store) and get me a model plane?" I, trying to teach him thrift, replied, "Why don't you save your money? Why, it was Ben Franklin himself who said 'A penny saved is a penny earned.' " My son's reply came quickly, "Oh, in that case, let's go to M. E. Moses. He didn't say that." Being a typical mother and thinking this story was cute, I sent it to Paul Crume, beloved columnist for the Dallas Morning News. He thought it was cute too and published it.

M. E. Moses may not be quoted as much as Benjamin Franklin, but he certainly was a master merchant. He and his wife opened their first store in Paducah, Texas, in 1924. In a building, twelve feet by forty feet, they displayed $1,500 worth of stock. They did so well in this spot that they were able to open another store in Quanah, Texas, where the company offices and warehouse were established. M. E. Moses stayed in Quanah until 1935, and then the company moved to Dallas. Store number eleven was opened in downtown

Dallas. Business boomed and more and more stores were opened all over Texas. There are 43 operating today.

In 1957, the central warehouse was moved to Oak Cliff. This building offered 40,000 feet for all the merchandise. In 1969, an additional 20,000 square feet was added, so during the days when the dime stores were disappearing, M. E. Moses was growing. The motto of the store still stands. "No sale is complete until the customer is absolutely satisfied." This means that any customer can obtain a refund or exchange on any purchase, no matter how small.

The Moses family made certain that the stores were always a vital part of the community. The firm's banking is always with the local banks. The stores only employ local sales people including the manager and assistant manager. And to add to it all, Mrs. Marie Moses is till working in the business that she and her husband started almost 70 years ago.

DR. PEPPER

Wade B. Morrison was born in Christianburg, Virginia, August 19, 1852. He attended school there and later went to the Philadelphia College of Pharmacy where he received his Doctor of Pharmacy degree. He also studied in Baltimore. As a young man, Wade worked at a drug store in Rural Retreat, Virginia. This drug store was owned by a local physician, Dr. Charles T. Pepper. The doctor had a beautiful daughter who frequented her father's drug store. Morrison was smitten with her, and eventually the two young people were in love. Dr. Pepper objected to their amorous feelings. The doctor felt that they were too young to be in love, and he also thought that Morrison showed no promise of being able to support a doctor's daughter. Dr. Pepper urged young Morrison to get out of town — out of the state. This he did. In fact, Morrison went as far as Austin, Texas. There he worked at Tobin Drug Store. In 1876, he moved to Round Rock, Texas, where he worked at another Tobin Drug Store. In this hill country town, he met and married a lovely girl, Carrie B. Jeffress. It just so happened that while Morrison was in Round Rock he witnessed the shooting of Sam Bass. Sam and his gang robbed the bank at Round Rock, but they didn't get far. The Bass gang were apprehended by the Texas Rangers who had received advance warning about the robbery. The rather staid druggest from Virginia, stood in awe of such wildness that did exist in the West. Nevertheless, the young druggist loved Texas, and eventually moved to Waco, Texas, where he joined John W. Castles. Their drug store was first known as Castles and Morrison, but when Morrison bought out the whole thing, it was called Morrison's Old Corner Drug Store. This first store was located at Fourth and Austin. Later the store moved to quarters adjacent to the Amicable Building. Morrison was in business in Waco for forty-two years. Because he held the doctorate in pharmacy, he was called *Dr. Morrison*. He could have easily supported that young doctor's daughter in Virginia, but it was too late to think of that now.

Dr. Morrison hired a young phamacist, Charles Courtice Alderton to work with him at the Old Corner Drug Store. Alderton was born in New York, June 21, 1857. He received his early schooling in England and was graduated from a college in Suffolk. Eventually, he came home to reside with his parents in Brooklyn, New York. Then he moved to Texas.

Charles Alderton graduated from the University of Texas Medical School in Galveston, but he decided not to practice medicine but rather to be a pharmacist. In 1884, he married Lillie E. Walker of Galveston and then moved to Waco where he accepted the job as pharmacist at the Old Corner Drug Store. Here, this well educated man doubled as pharmacist and soda jerk. Because of his experience and background in research, when he was behind the soda fountain, he often experimented with different flavors for sodas. Alderton noticed that the patrons often were turned off by the usual flavors — strawberry, cherry, orange, lemon, sarsaparilla, etc. He began to try different combinations. Remember that Alderton was educated in England, and the English probably had more to do with the origin and development of carbonated beverages than any other people. Also, he was very inventive by nature, so he loved to experiment. Experiment he did! In fact, he came up with a very unusual formula for a soft drink.

Here's where we go into the third act of our soda saga. Enter — Robert Sherman Lazenby. This gentleman was born in Johnson County, Texas, September 12, 1866. His blood line went back to the Virginia Cavaliers. His family held a land grant in the Old Dominion of Virginia from King George III himself! Lazenby's father left Virginia and went to Alabama where he married Lucy Goodwin. Miss Goodwin was from the family that received the Circle A rights for their Texas cattle from the Spanish. Robert later used that Circle A as a brand for the Ginger Ale that he compounded.

Robert Lazenby was always interested in chemistry and studied pharmacy in Paris, Texas. At age 18 he introduced Circle A Ginger Ale which was the finest of that type of soda in the nation. He started his bottle works in a small plant in Waco in 1884. It was in this plant that he began to produce the syrup created by Alderton in Morrison's drug store. It was called Dr. Pepper, obviously named by Morrison for the doctor who had thrown him out of Virginia. Legend has it that Morrison went back and married the doctor's daughter. We know that isn't tue.

When Southern Methodist University was founded in 1911, R. H. Lazenby was instrumental in getting the funds for the school. Later SMU was to receive even more money from Lazenby's daughter, Mrs. Virginia O'Hara. Over a million dollars went to the chemistry department. It was so appropriate that the new headquarters for Dr. Pepper be built in Dallas next door to SMU. This building was begun in 1947. I remember my father wondering why they chose to build out in the country. "Can you imagine? They're building that plant out on Greenville Road — past Mockingbird — out in the country!" I remember riding my bicycle out there to see what was going on in the country. Well, presently, the old building is for sale, and it's almost considered downtown property.

Dr. Pepper has always had terrific advertising. The most memorable, of course, was the Dr. Pepper Clock with the dominate hours — ten, two and four. Dr. Walter H. Eddy, Ph.D., published a book in 1944, *The Liquid Bite.* In this book he supposedly proved his theory that every human being needed to drink something sweet in between meals to keep up the energy. Dr. Pepper quickly moved in with "Drink a Bite to Eat — Ten, Two and Four!" The timing was perfect, since everyone was working overtime for the war effort.

Dr. Pepper has been served cold — "Frosty, Man, Frosty," and has been served *Hot!* Wesby Reed Parker, president of the company in the 60s came up with the *hot* idea. Regardless of how it's served, Dr. Pepper has always been Dallas' answer to Atlanta's Coca Cola!

94

LOUIE KIMPLE AND WAX PAPER

Louie C. Kimple started as a salesman for the R. J. Reynolds Tobacco Company — a salesman who never smoked himself. As he made money he invested it wisely and survived the crash of 1929 — a true genius with money. He was able to spot the weaknesses and strengths of the market — a rare gift!

In the early 1920s, Louie Kimple with three other men bought out the Texas Paper Company. The company at that time was trying out a system of making paper with cotton, but it just never worked. There was also some experimentation with waxing paper. This process was working, and to this Louie Kimple gave his attention. He called the company the Dixie Wax Paper Company always pointing out the grammatical error in the name. It really should have been Dixie *Waxed* Paper.

The company at that time was in a garage near Fair Park, just off Exposition Avenue. One of the investors was extremely mechanical. He worked diligently to perfect the machine that waxed the paper. The wax was melted in a large vat and the paper was run through it. The paper was then rolled and ready for sales.

Timing was always just perfect for Louie. Also in the early 1920s ladies began to buy more bread, not bake it at home. With all this bread being baked in factories and shipped everywhere, packaging had to guarantee freshness. What better way to promise complete freshness than to package in wax paper? Louie Kimple had the wax paper!

He would put the rolls of the special paper in an old Model T Ford and sell it to all the bakeries that were beginning to boom here in the Dallas area. Sales were brisk. The company grew and moved to a larger place across from Lake Cliff at Zang and Colorado.

In 1928, again with perfect timing, Mr. Kimple bought out a company in Memphis, Tennessee, the Sani-Wax Paper Company. Now, Louie had businesses going at both ends of the country. With his great business sense and again with good timing, Louie Kimple diversified his paper company. In the early 30s, Frito Corn Chips were created which ushered in the age of snack foods. This type of goods needed special packaging, so the company produced preformed bags that were perfect for all of the snack foods that were to come on the market.

After World War II, with business booming, Dixico Inc., the

new name for the company, opened plants in Mexico City, New Jersey and Northern California.

Also after the war, plastic became the all purpose material. The company then began to manufacture plastic tubes for toothpaste and other products of this nature. When automobiles began to use heavy duty plastic accessories, the company was ready to manufacture these products. Dixico bought out plastic companies in Ohio, California, and New Jersey. Today, Dixico, Inc. is at 1300 Polk Street. It's housed in a building that won all sorts of architectural awards for its designer, David Braden.

MARY C AND MARY KAY

We've all heard of the wicked stepmother. Well, Mary Crowley had one. When Mary was eighteen months old, her mother died and she was then cared for by her grandparents. They adored the little girl and she thrived on their love. However, her father remarried and Mary was then under the care of her wicked stepmother. She was mean! Mary saved money for a special coat. Her stepmother agreed to order the coat, but instead, kept the money and got Mary an old coat at the Good Will. With this sort of treatment, Mary was certainly thrilled when she was once again taken to live with her grandparents.

Nevertheless, in order to have a real home of her own, Mary married the minute she got out of high school. Two children, Don and Ruth, were born soon after. The marriage didn't survive, but Mary surely did. When she realized that she had the two kids to support, she immediately set out to find some marketable skills. She discovered that she loved to sell and that she had a real knack for it. She worked in a store, and then she discovered another available market for herself — home sales of Stanley Products. It was here that she met Mary Kay Ash. Mary Kay encouraged her friend, Mary Crowley, to continue in direct home sales. The two ladies were extremely successful — so successful that they both branched out on their own.

Mary C. found a distributor for home accessories. This is when she got the idea to sell these home accessories through home parties. She just knew it would work. An active member of the First Baptist Church, Mary knew a very enterprising young attorney,

Ralph Baker, who helped her get the money to start her company, Home Interiors. Eventually, there were parties in homes all over the United States, and through these parties, the sales soared. Mary made a lot of money, but Mary always gave a lot of money away. Her "girls" that conducted the home parties were always rewarded in big ways — grocery shopping sprees, trips, cash prizes. Mary always gave the Lord credit for her success, so she gave generously to her church. The Mary C Building is a useful and appreciated part of the First Baptist Church complex.

Mary's venturesome and resourceful son, Don Carter, used the family's money wisely in several other business enterprises. He's best known for his ownership of and big interest in the Dallas basketball team — fondly called the Mavericks.

Now, while Mary C. was working hard with her company, Mary Kay was working just as hard with her business. These ladies are similar in many ways. They just sold different products. While Mary C. was thinking of homes and home decorations, Mary Kay was thinking of beauty rituals and cosmetics. She began her quest for the very best in beauty products that could be sold through direct sales .in the home — not at home parties, but home demonstrations. Ladies could come for complete make overs and what woman doesn't want to be made over? Sales boomed for Mary Kay.

Mary Kay too married very young and had three children. Her husband went off to World War II. The marriage was shakey before he left, and when he returned it was finished. She too had to support a family and this was when she got involved with Stanley Products — selling at home. She too thought of selling as an art and she definitely had the talent. Her business is in the family today, in that her son is president of the company.

Mary Kay takes care of her "girls" too. They are given pink Cadillacs, trips, diamonds.

Mary Kay too gives the Lord credit for all of her accomplishments. Prestonwood Baptist Church received her tithe, and this church was able to grow a little more because of her contributions.

These two ladies, Mary C and Mary Kay, had virtually nothing when they started their businesses. They worked hard and they prospered. Fortunately, they have shared their prosperity with the City of Dallas.

TEXAS INSTRUMENTS

On May 6, 1930, the charter was drawn up to establish the Geophysical Service Incorporated. The country was reeling from a depression. It was the worst time ever to start a business, but J. C. Karcher and Eugene McDermott didn't know this. Another young man was unaware of the risk, so he left his job as engineer with Alcoa to join these two. His name — Erik Jonsson. Others joined — W. C. Edwards, Jr., Chris Elston, Everett Stanfill, Alfred P. Morel, Kenneth E. Burg, Cecil H. Green, and Norris Walsh. GSI was located at 6000 Lemon Avenue, and in spite of the depression, the business flourished. The company led in oil finds everywhere, and by 1940, the business was operating all over the world. "GSI was the first independent Geophysical contracting firm to specialize in the reflection seismic method of geophysical exploration for petroleum and other minerals." Whatever that means, this bunch could do it.

After the war, in 1946, the company diversified by adding electronic systems manufacturing. By 1952, they entered the transistor business with a new name, Texas Instruments. The patents were registered as fast as a human could do the job. There were no computers then, *until* — 1958, when TI came up with the integrated circuit, the basis of all modern electronics. By 1961, they had a miniature computer on the market. Then came the printer, the calculator, the data terminal, the memory, and on and on. In 1981, TI published computer language and now, if you don't know what I'm talking about, you are to be pitied. In fact, that's why I'm feeling sorry for myself. I don't think I understand what I've just written.

LTV

During World War II the metroplex had its share of warfare industry. There was North American Aviation, a gigantic plant that was strictly off limits to everyone except employees during the war. I remember one "open house" that the big company staged for the citizens of Dallas. I got to go through this mega plant that was producing planes, rockets, etc. — all sorts of secret weapons.

When the war was over a Texas entrepreneur, James J. Ling, who had started Ling Electric Company in the late 1940s with

$6,000 he had earned on some quick real estate deals, merged his company with Temco Electronics. In 1961, Ling merged again with Chance Vought. This company named for Chauncy M. "Chance" Vought, an aircraft designer and pilot, moved its manufacturing facilities to the old North American Aviation plant in 1948. With the Ling merger, the name emerged, Ling, Temco, Vought: LTV. Ling was able to complete this massive mix despite objections form the justice department.

ELECTRONIC DATA SYSTEMS

Ross Perot was born in 1930, Texarkana, Texas. He attended Texarkana Junior College, was a midshipman at Annapolis in 1949, and in 1953, received his Bachelor of Science Degree. He left the navy in 1957 to work for IBM. His creativity was stifled there, so in 1962, he founded his own company, Electronic Data Systems, the pioneer in computer services. His company became the data processing department for the largest insurance companies and the biggest banks. It's the world's largest data processing for credit unions. Through the years, Mr. Perot has mastered almost everything he has taken on — General Motors, Iran, the Texas School Board — to name a few.

LOCAL MILKMEN — CABELL AND METZGER

In 1977, North Dallas High School was 50 years old, and I was asked to put together a program for the occasion. The illustrious former Mayor and US Congressman, Earl Cabell, was one of the distinguished alumni of North Dallas. He was on hand at the celebration to say a few words.

Cabell pointed out that during the depression when nothing seemed to go in the business world, he opened his dairy stores all over Dallas. They prospered. Cabells Ice Cream Parlors were the most popular spots in town. I frequented the one at 1801 Greenville. My good high school buddy, Betty Wilson, has an antique store at that location now, Granny B's Antiques, corner of Greenville and Lewis.

Earl Cabell came from a very active family to say the least. His father, General W. L. Cabell, came to Dallas after the Civil War and eventually served as Mayor of the city. Then his son, Ben Cabell, also served as Mayor. Then, Ben's son, Earl, served as Mayor and went on to the U.S. Congress, 5th District. There is a large federal building bearing the Earl Cabell name in the center of downtown Dallas. This family was definitely a cornerstone for our city.

We kids loved Cabells Milk, but we also patronized another dairy, Metzgers. Each day, we'd wait for the friendly Metzgers Dairy horse to pull up for milk delivery at the back door step. In other words, I grew up knowing a milkman — a man from Metzgers Dairies who delivered milk to the house in a horse drawn wagon.

Jacob Metzger left Switzerland and arrived in Canada in 1873. In 1875, he wended his way to Dallas. Here he worked for Chris Moser, who was a dairyman. By 1889, Jacob Metzger decided to go into the dairy business himself. He rented a farm which bordered on North Carroll, Haskell, and Ross. On this spread, he kept 30 cows. Later he bought land on Holmes Street (South Central) and expanded his dairy service. Metzger was the first dairyman to use bottles for home delivery. This happened in 1906. He was the first to pasteurize milk in Dallas. In 1930, Metzgers Dairy was the first to put rubber tires on the delivery trucks, making the wagons easier to pull. This helped the horse a lot. No wonder the horse was so friendly when we kids greeted him. He wasn't working all that hard!

Eventually, Metzgers Dairy began delivering milk in refrigerated trucks, and then they didn't deliver at all. Why should they? Everyone had a car! The sons, David and Carl, took over and on March 2, 1984, Metzgers sold out to Borden.

Jacob and his wife are buried in Grove Hill Cemetery next to my grandfather and grandmother. Just think! There lies the bread and butter of Dallas!

FRITO LAY

One afternoon in 1932, Elmer Doolin went into a small San Antonio cafe for lunch. At this time the country, actually the whole world, was in a deep, dark depression, and Mr. Doolin was feeling this economic pinch from all sides. His little ice cream business was suffering from a price war which was going on in San Antonio. He was getting the double whammy! Things were bad all over — especially for him, he thought. Doolin ordered a nickel sandwich and then decided to really splurge. He bought a sack of corn chips for five cents. This was the greatest investment Elmer Doolin ever made in his whole life. In the package, he discovered the tastiest corn chip of all time. It was made from corn meal masa, which was the same dough that the Mexicans for centuries had been mixing together to make their bread — tortillas. He loved the chip and inquired about the recipe. The owner of the cafe who made the chips was anxious to return to Mexico. So he said, "For $100 I'll give you the recipe, the 19 accounts I have, and the equipment you need to make the chip." The equipment was an ancient potato ricer.

Elmer Doolin got the $100. He borrowed it from his mother. She sold her wedding ring for the cash. This is legend, but it possibly could be true. Nevertheless, Elmer set up operations in his mother's kitchen and sold the chips out of the back of his Model T Ford. The profit ran up to $2 a day.

In a couple of months, Doolin moved his operations to Dallas, where he made the corn chips in his garage. This garage could be considered a plant. That's why Dallas claims the birth of the corn chip — not San Antonio. By the way, Doolin called his chip a Frito.

Meanwhile, the same year, 1932, Nashville, Tennessee, Herman Lay was the distributor of Barrett Food Products. He owned a Model A Ford and used his car to distribute sandwiches. Then he began to sell pop corn and eventually potato chips. By, 1937, Mr. Lay had fifteen other distributors working for him. He had a full-fledged snack food enterprise.

Timing is so important for the building of a business, and these two men couldn't want for more perfect timing. The super market was emerging. World War II started and the demand for snack food was rising. War plant workers needed something special in their lunch pails. The men overseas needed snacks between battles. Fritos were in demand along with Lay Potato Chips.

After the war, there was more business for both gentlemen. In 1959, Elmer Doolin died leaving his snack food empire to the corporation. In 1961 the H. W. Lay Company and the Frito Company joined together. In 1965, they went together with Pepsi Cola. Today, it's a great big booming business with corporate headquarters in Dallas!

101

LET'S EAT

Louis Wagner's grocery store was built in 1868 on the southeast corner of Main and Jefferson. My grandfather's bakery was on the northeast corner of Main and Jefferson. My mother grew up with the Wagner kids, because they lived over the grocery store just like my mother lived over the bakery. For some time, Wagner's Grocery Store was the only grocery store downtown. Of course, more stores opened as the town grew.

When I was a kid growing up near what is now called Lower Greenville, our grocery store was Clark and Johnson, located in the 2000 block of Greenville across from the Arcadia Theatre. I remember Mr. Clark so well — he delivered! He was friendly and cordial at the store, but he was always ready to bring your groceries to your house just in case you couldn't make it to the store. In those days, everyone just had one car if that many, so when the weather was bad, many housewives couldn't walk to the store. Mr. Clark was willing and able to accommodate these ladies. Later on, he added a deli and a cafeteria for those who wanted to eat out.

Today, Dallas has some very accommodating grocers — wholesale and retail. Here are a few with whom I've had some dealings.

TOM THUMB

In the early 1900s, A. W. Cullum worked for a wholesale grocery company, Bradford and Company, at Pacific and Akard. Jesse James worked there too. Jesse really got around in those days! In 1919, Mr. Cullum opened his own wholesale grocery at the corner of Turtle Creek and Cedar Springs. Eventually, he opened some retail grocery stores, and because he had the smallest chain in the city he called his stores Tom Thumb.

The Cullums were in charge of the company until 1966. It was then that Jack Evans, Sr., astute business man and one time Mayor of Dallas, joined the company as President. Later, Jack Evans, Jr. joined the firm right after he graduated from the University of North Texas, and he has taken the reins.

I do some work for Tom Thumb. They have this marvelous program, PARTY FARE. Tom Thumb and their sponsors furnish the food and the fun for any non-profit organization that is willing

102

to furnish the eaters. All of the money from the ticket sales for the dinner stays with the organization that is sponsoring the dinner. I have a great time as entertainer. People often ask, "What does Tom Thumb get out of it?" The answer is simple — ME. I promote the food. Hopefully everyone will rush out and shop at Tom Thumb and buy the products of the sponsoring companies. It's a great advertising gimmick. Cherie January Stowe, home economist for Tom Thumb, started the whole program.

MINYARDS

On February 12, 1932, A. W. "Eck" Minyard bought a little grocery store at 6015 Lindsley, so his brothers, Henry and Buddy, could have a place to work when they came home from school. Eck kept his job at the post office so he could pay off the loan on the store. He put $10 down and was paying $2 a week, so it was necessary to have an income to make these payments. The little store was called The Home Town Grocer because the Minyards extended credit to anyone in that East Dallas neighborhood that needed it. When World War II came, the boys went off to serve and hung a sign in the window of the store, "Closed until Hitler's funeral."

When the war was over, the boys saw to it that the business grew with the country. Minyards still remained the home town grocer even though the whole operation was much bigger than one little store.

The business today is still in the hands of the Minyard family. Two daughters, Liz and Gretchen, are in charge now!

THE SCHEPPS

Two of my favorite people in Dallas are George and Evelyn Schepps. Evelyn is a beauty, and George is a character. It seems that George has always been a character. A school mate was quoted as saying, "Julius (brother) grew up to be a fine businessman, and George grew up to be George."

Regardless, their parents were in the bakery business. Father, Joe, and mother, Jennie, ran the whole operation. Their son, Julius, lived the life of a model son. He delivered newspapers as a kid, grew up to take over the family business, and then turn it into something much bigger than Papa ever dreamed of. George, in the

103

meantime, was a bat boy for the New York Giants, 1909. When he came back to Dallas, he went into the liquor business. One friend pointed out that "George sold hooch before it was legal." Nevertheless, in 1934, he opened a brewery and the business thrived. He even had his own brand of beer. Because he still loved baseball, George owned the Dallas Rebels. Really, it was a training camp for the big leagues. He'd train the players and sell them to the majors. Eventually, in 1948, he sold the Rebels to Dick Burnett.

I have always enjoyed being in the company of George Schepps. He has often invited me to come down to the warehouse and entertain his troops, and believe me, his employees make a good audience for my act.

Julius Schepps went on in the bakery business, the dairy business, the grocery business. Dallas honored him with an expressway and the Jewish people built a recreational center on Park Lane, naming it after Julius. Twenty-five years ago, I taught a class in theatre at the Julius Schepps Center. I had two very talented kids in that class under my tutelage. One was Laurel Ornish who emceed a classical music program on WRR. Her mother, Natalie, wrote a fine book, *Pioneer Jewish Texans*. Son, Dean Ornish, also in the class, is a reknowned doctor who has written two best sellers, *Dr. Dean's Program for Reversing Heart Disease* and *Stress, Diet, and Your Heart.*

WICKER FISH AND POULTRY
— now a part of Sysco Food Systems

In 1929, D. E. Wicker, Sr. came to Dallas and decided to open the Wicker Fish and Poultry Company. He would sell fish and fowl wholesale to the grocers in the area. Wicker had been associated with a grocery store in Fort Worth, but he felt that Dallas would be the best place to go into business. His company, located on Cadiz Street, prospered. When D. E. Wicker, Jr., was in Baylor University finishing his medical degree, he worked one summer for his father. He fell in love with fish and poultry and decided that he preferred fish and poultry to practicing medicine. This love for the business was genuine, because he was very close to becoming a doctor when he decided to join his daddy and the fish and the fowl. Regardless, D. E., Jr. joined the company and it continued to prosper. Eventually, the plant was moved to the corner of Gaston and

Oakland. There is no more Wicker Fish and Poultry. The company is now part of the giant Sysco Food Systems. Grandson, David Wicker, is a big part of this company which offers prepared and processed foods. One can see Sysco delivery trucks everywhere. This company is able to outfit any restaurant with any need. They have everything from soup to nuts — from salads to tables and chairs. They will furnish anything and everything one might need in the restaurant business.

LET'S EAT OUT

When my last kid left home, I blew out the pilot light. I quit cooking. So naturally, without any home cooking, my husband and I had to find nourishment elsewhere. Jack sent me a Valentine last year that read, "I'm sending you those three little words you love to hear — Let's eat out!" Here are some eating establishments that have always meant a lot to me. The first two no longer exist, but I'll always remember them. The others mentioned are going strong.

THE TORCH

When I was a Girl Scout leader, I always took my dear little troup to the Torch restaurant to see the treasures from Greece that were on display there. We also heard some fascinating stories of the home land from the owner of the restaurant, Victor H. Semos. Mr. Semos came to the United States and opened the Torch, a restaurant featuring Greek food, when Dallas was a city without ethnic restaurants. This vibrant and enthusiastic gentleman opened his restaurant on Davis Street, and stayed in business for 36 years. The Torch closed in 1984.

Victor Semos had a lot of help in running the restaurant from his son, Chris Semos, who served our state as a legislator and who is now County Commissioner.

Because Victor knew and loved Greek history so much, he published a newspaper regularly — The Torch. In this paper he revealed some of his famous recipes. He would list the private parties that were going to be held at the restaurant, and then he would offer some Greek history for the patrons who wanted some inside information on the Greeks.

Victor Semos went home to Greece often and he always

brought back more treasures of his home land. These beautiful relics were always on display at the restaurant for customers to see.

In 1970, a true Greek tragedy took place. The Torch burned, but Semos was quick to rebuild. He added an International dining room that was extremely popular for all sorts of parties, meetings, and gatherings. The Torch is gone, and I really miss it. Wonder where the little Girl Scouts go to study Greece?

SIVILS DRIVE INN

When I was teaching at Dallas Baptist University, I called the role at the beginning of the semester. There was the name, Bob Sivils. "Are you related to the infamous Sivils Drive In?" I asked. "Well, my daddy owns it and I wash dishes if that counts," was the answer. Bob Sivils graduated from Dallas Baptist and today he is a vice-president of an insurance agency, The Bankers Assurance. He gives me half credit for his success. "You and that drive in got me through college."

In 1934, J. D. and Louise Sivils opened a couple of restaurants in Houston. The automobile was getting more and more popular and attainable, so Louise suggested that they have a restaurant where one could drive up and a waitress could come out to the car. J. D. went with the idea. Louise created the name Drive Inn. It was under copyright for years. Please note the two N's. That was her original spelling.

Well, J. D. cooked, because that was what he loved to do, and Louise groomed the girls, because that was what she loved to do. Her girls were not just going to walk out to the car, they were going to strut. Louise then decided they would strut out in majorette costumes. One of her girls was Kay Williams who later married Clark Gable and had his only child.

Since these were the big cigarette smoking days, Chesterfield used Sivils Drive Inn for the background of one of their ads. Finally, this unique restaurant ended up on the cover of *Life* magazine, February 26, 1940. Now, this all happened in Houston. In 1943, Sivils Drive Inn opened at 3500 Fort Worth Avenue and there it operated until May 1967. At one time, when the establishment stayed open 24 hours a day, there were 105 girls on the payroll.

Well, the days of the car hop are pretty well over. Oops, pardon me, Louise! I didn't mean to say car hop. She called them curb girls.

THE HIGHLAND PARK CAFETERIA

Sallie Goodman came down to Dallas from Oklahoma to visit some friends. She was a widow with six boys and one girl to support. Obviously, she had a lot of responsibility, but she had this feeling she was going to make it — this dream! Sallie could cook! Her friends suggested that she stay in Dallas and start cooking, so she took their advice. On August 24, 1925, with this dream in her heart, Sallie opened a little cafeteria on Knox Street between Travis and the railroad tracks. There were 13 stools and 8 tables, and she called it the Highland Park Cafeteria. Dewey, one of the sons, waited the tables, and Sallie cooked.

The next year, 1926, Dewey married Carolyn and the two of them helped Mama Goodman with the cafeteria. Sallie's business prospered so much that she enlarged by moving across Knox Street in the block between McKinney and Cole. The Knox Street area was beginning to grow at that time. There was a movie theatre and Wier's Furniture Company opened for business. Sallie soon had the most popular eating place in town. Today in the new location on the corner of Knox and Cole, if you want lunch, better get in line at 10:45. If you want dinner, better get in line at 4:45. If you're late, then you're in the longest line in town.

WYATTS CAFETERIAS

At the age of 10, Earl Wyatt worked as a grocery store delivery boy. His family lived in Waco, and there as a young man he managed a grocery store, Cash Mercantile. In 1917, Earl enlisted in the army and went off to World War I. When he came home from the war, he decided to live in Dallas, where he began managing one of the Clarence Saunders Stores, Piggley Wiggley. Clarence Saunders was the ingenious grocer who, in his first little store in Memphis, Tennessee, created aisles. Until Saunders built his aisles, people just roamed through the grocery stores buying just what they needed. He arranged his store in aisles, so that everyone had to pass *by* everything in order to *buy* anything. Customers

107

began to buy on sight. In other words, Saunders initiated impulse buying. Unfortunately, Saunders went broke and Earl Wyatt and his brother Edwin bought 15 of the Saunders stores here in Dallas. The brothers renamed their stores, Home Town Grocery.

Earl, being a thrifty type guy, never allowed anything to go to waste. If there were potatoes left over, or if there were some apples that wouldn't sell, then he hired a cook to make potato salad and apple cobbler. He sold the cooked food. When he added barbecue, lo and behold, he had a restaurant — or better yet, a cafeteria on Elm Street. In 1931, Wyatts Cafeteria opened in the Lakewood Shopping Center and in Oak Cliff. Then one opened on Greenville where the antique mall is today. During World War II, Wyatt got the contract to feed the workers at the war plants that were operating in the metroplex. This was a very good deal for him!

THE BLUE FRONT

At 1105 Elm, in 1877, the Blue Front Saloon opened. The proprietor sold so much beer and spirits that he could afford to serve free lunches. The food must have been good, because the saloon became a restaurant. The bread was good, that's for sure, because it was furnished by the baker, William Schliepake. His bakery was at 1710 S. Harwood. After twenty-five years of baking, Schliepake sold the bakery and bought the Blue Front. For years and years this was the most popular eating place in downtown Dallas. At noon, blue collars, white collars — anyone with or without a collar, ate at the Blue Front. By the way, for years, only men were allowed in the restaurant. Not so today. Everyone downtown eats at the Blue Front regularly or irregularly. It's still a popular place. Mrs. Schliepake was at the cash register until she died at 81 years of age.

The original Blue Front was torn down to make way for what is now Renaissance Tower. For two years the restaurant operated at Field and Commerce under Jack Ruby's Carousel Club. Now, at 1310 Elm Street, the Blue Front is underground. When the restaurant was 100 years old, Mayor Folsom declared October 22, 1977, Blue Front Day!

EL FENIX

Miguel "Mike" Martinez was born in 1890, Hacienda de Potreno in Nuevo Leon, Mexico. At the age of seven, he was driving the burros to the mines and by age fifteen, he was working in the mines. The young man always had the dream of coming to the United States, so when he was nineteen years old he escaped from his very torturous existence and somehow managed to get to Dallas. He married Faustina Parros, and in order to support his wife and his family, he acquired a job as dishwasher at the Oriental Hotel. When he wasn't working, he was watching the chef. One evening, the chef was not at the hotel and Mike stepped in and covered for him very nicely. Too nicely! When the chef returned, he was so jealous of the young lad, he had him fired. Mike didn't grieve long over the job. In fact, he came up with this thought that guided him all of his life. "Don't look too long at the door that has been closed, for if you do, you'll miss the one that is opening."

By 1918, Mike had enough money to open his own restaurant at Griffin and McKinney. He called it El Fenix. Eventually, he opened a larger one just across the street from the first one. Today, El Fenix Restaurants are all over town.

One of the Martinez sons married Anita, a beautiful girl, whose family had been in Dallas for years. In 1969, Anita Martinez ran for the city council, won, and became the first Hispanic to serve on the Dallas council. She had come a long way from being that rather shy little girl born on Pearl Street!

EL CHICO

Those people at the Kaufman County fair in 1926 really experienced a terrific treat. Mama Cuellar and her boys were there selling their delicious tamales. Mama's boys, Frank, Alfred, Mack, Gilbert, and Willie Jack, peddled the very best in Mexican creations — the perfect tamale. They went to fairs, markets, parks, anywhere with their delectable cuisine. The boys and Mama finally had enough money to open a restaurant in Dallas on the corner of Oak Lawn and Lemmon in 1940 which they called El Chico. It was such a popular place that they decided to open another restaurant in the Lakewood shopping center. This was in 1946. The one on Oak Lawn is no more, but the one in Lakewood is always filled with hungry and satisfied eaters. The Lakewood folk loved the food and the Cuellars so much, there is a memorial in front of the restaurant dedicated to Gilbert Cuellar, Sr. from all of his friends in East Dallas.

109

LITTLE GUS

Back in the days when men were men, women were women, and hamburgers were greasy and great, the spot, 1916 Greenville Avenue, that filled the bill for any really true hamburger lover was Little Gus. That great red meat was fried in grease, and then the bun was warmed in that same grease. Pickles and mustard were added and the whole thing was like manna from heaven. In those days, no one was concerned about cholesterol or fat or anything. We were concerned about Hitler and Tojo, but we certainly weren't concerned about what we ate.

The great thing is that Little Gus is still serving delicious food. What I like to do is pick up a book or a magazine at Shakespear's Book Store, go next door to Little Gus, and read and eat.

In 1939 Jimmy Mantzuranis opened the Garden Food Store just down the street from where Little Gus is now. He'd go to the farmer's market and get the best vegetables for his customers. We lived on Sears Street then. My daddy sold that property just behind the Arcadia Theatre to the government. They built a post office there. But, before this, we ate a lot of Jimmy's vegetables.

Jimmy decided to go in the restaurant business — bought and opened Little Gus. In 1947, Jimmy ordered his bride from his home land which was Greece. Amalia arrived, sight unseen. They married and they have been married ever since. Jimmy is 84 years old now, and he and his bride eat lunch every day at Little Gus. That says a lot for the food he has served through the years.

TOLBERT'S CHILI PARLORS
— One Dallas Center and the West End

I have an autographed copy of the first edition of Frank X. Tolbert's *An Informal History of Texas*. It's a rare book today, and it was a rare book in 1951, the day it was published. This book gives the "real dope" on our great State of Texas.

No one could spin a tale like Frank Tolbert. He was a sports editor for papers in Lubbock, Amarillo, Wichita Falls, and Fort Worth. During World War II he was managing editor and combat correspondent for *The Leatherneck*, magazine of the Marine Corps.

He was known in Dallas for his column "Tolbert's Texas"

which appeared weekly in the *Dallas Morning News.* Later, Tolbert became known for his chili. He won every chili cook-out that was ever sponsored. Tolbert is telling tales in heaven today, and we're enjoying his chili. It's the greatest.

BARBECUE!

On February 13, 1910, a barbecue stand opened on Centre Street, Oak Cliff. The owner and super cook was Elias Bryan. The barbecue was great and so was business. Many barbecue fans thought Mr. Elias Bryan could support a family just on the aroma from that spicy barbecue sauce alone, much less on the taste of the melt-in-the-mouth beef. He had a son named William Jennings Bryan I, who was fondly called "Red." Elias gave all his culinary secrets and skills to his son, so on February 13, 1930, Red Bryan opened his barbecue business on Jefferson in an old quonset hut. This was located right across the street from where Sears was to open their giant store. Red served good barbecue, but he also was a public servant. He was elected to the city council on February 13, 1947. In the meantime, the business thrived, so the quonset hut was replaced by a fine building. By this time there was William Jennings Bryan II, fondly called "Sonny." He too was into barbecue. All was well, but eventually, things were going to change. In 1957, Oak Cliff voted to go dry. The Bryans felt they needed the money from the sale of beer in order to truly make a substantial profit. So, on February 13, 1958, Sonny Bryan opened his restaurant on Inwood Road. It is going great guns, and soon there will be a Sonny Bryan's Barbecue at the West End.

What about William Jennings Bryan III. Well, he's not into barbecue. He's a Methodist minister. Grace Methodist Church is very fortunate to have this dynamic preacher as their leader. This is a very old East Dallas church that is now in an area where several ethnic groups reside. Also, it is in the midst of a big restoration tract. The large two story homes are being renovated and young families are moving in. Grace Methodist and Reverend Bryan minister to all the needs of this diverse neighborhood.

CHAPTER VI

Some Area Personalities

F. M. OLIVER — FIRST CITIZEN OF OAK CLIFF

In 1887, T. L. Marsalis purchased 2,000 acres of rocky cliffs and fields south of the Trinity River from Judge William Hord. This land extended from what is now Colorado northward and eastward to Beckley Avenue.

On November 1, 1887, F. N. Oliver, a journalist, purchased the first parcel of land from T. L. Marsalis, thus becoming the first citizen of Oak Cliff. Oliver opened a newspaper publishing business, eventually publishing 15,000 copies of the *Oak Cliff Sunday Weekly*. This newspaper was the first in Texas to use paper made in the immediate area. The Texas Paper Mill was the supplier.

F. N. Oliver was the eighth child of Daniel and Jane Oliver. His father, Dan, had a degree from Yale University and eventually went back to head the mathematics department at Yale. F. N. was born in Florence, Alabama, February 17, 1848. He went to public school there and learned to be a printer. Seeking adventure, he came to Texas, met and married Miss Mary E. Cogbaron in Cold Springs, Texas, December 13, 1868. In 1874, F. N. published his first newspaper in Texas, which was the first daily that Denton County ever enjoyed.

He then moved to Lewisville and published the *Lewisville Headlight*. Later, he published a paper in Pilot Point. Finally, he came to Oak Cliff and published the *Oak Cliff Sunday Weekly*. Here, F. N. became a charter member of the Dallas Chapter of the National Press Association.

F. N. Oliver didn't just give his life to the publishing business. He organized the Oak Cliff School System and with G. M Baker and F. M. Ewing, served as a trustee. He and his wife organized the first Sunday School in Oak Cliff, January 1, 1888, at the First Methodist Episcopal South Church. Then finally, this civic minded individual was elected the first Mayor of Oak Cliff.

The Olivers' first son was the first person born in Oak Cliff, June 20, 1889. F. N. wanted to name the child Cliff after the town, but the mother insisted that he be named Clifton. At this writing, Clifton is 102 years old and is living in Amarillo.

THE FIERY FRENCHMAN: CLEMENT LETOT

Before fighting became an organized sport, good fighters, in order to make any money with their strength and talent, traveled from small town to small town and challenged the toughest man there to a fight. Wagers were made on the outcome, and the traveling contender usually left with the victory and the purse. Whenever a professional fighter arrived in Dallas in the late nineteenth century and asked who was the toughest man in the county, he would be told, "The Frenchman, Letot!" Unfortunately for these wayfaring fighters, as long as Clement Letot would accept their challenges, they would leave defeated, disgraced, and penniless, for nobody could whip Clement Letot.

In later years the champion often told his grandchildren about the time a fighter approached him while he was plowing his field. He was using a double furrow plow, "I'm looking for a fight," said the visitor. "They tell me I can get one with a tough Frenchman named Letot. Know where I can find him? He ain't as tough as I am." Letot didn't answer right away. He first lifted the heavy plow with one arm and held it high in the air. "I'm that tough Frenchman, Letot, that you think you can beat," he replied, slowly lower-

113

ing the plow to the ground. The would-be competitor sneaked back into the hedges, hopped the Katy freight that ran by the Letot property, and was never seen again.

Clement Letot was born October 22, 1836, in the province of Burgundy, France, the son and grandson of men who had fought in the Napoleonic wars. In 1854, he enlisted in the French Navy and served as a machinist on a ship in the Black Sea during the Crimean War. In 1859, he jumped ship in New York and made his way to Chicago. There he worked as a machinist until he had enough money to buy 640 acres in LaSalle County, Illinois, where his parents had settled several years earlier. In 1861, he married Nathle Barnard, daughter of another French immigrant living in La Salle County; the couple eventually had nine children.

In 1876, Letot sold his land, piled all his belongings on an ox cart, and made the long journey to Dallas County. Here he bought 640 acres about nine miles northwest of the city of Dallas, and soon added another 470 acres. On a hill in the middle of his property he built a substantial residence, costing $4,000, with mantel, staircase, and front door imported from France. The site of the house is now occupied by Calvary Hill Cemetery. Wild game was so plentiful in the area that Letot used to brag that he could shoot all the ducks, doves, and rabbits he wanted while sitting on his front porch.

A small community, appropriately called Letot, soon grew up in the area. Clement Letot served as postmaster, owner and operator of the general store, and owner and operator of the cotton gin. In 1875, the Dallas and Wichita Railroad was built through the area, ending in Lewisville; Letot was the first stop out of Dallas.

Clement Letot was instrumental in building an interdenominational church for the town, which doubled as a schoolhouse. It was later annexed by the Dallas Independent School District and is still used for special programs.

Letot's strength was apparently matched by his obstinacy. Once, when he took his corn to market to sell, he became so infuriated over the low price offered that he dumped the entire load into the Trinity River. But he raised a responsible, hard-working family, some of whose descendants are still residents of Dallas.

Clement Letot died in 1907 and was buried in the family cemetery that now adjoins Calvary Hill on the north. In accordance with an old French tradition, his body was laid on a narrow bed which was lowered into an underground brick and concrete vault. A curved concrete cover was placed over the grave. His marker can still be seen today.

MAXIM GUILLOT, THE FIRST MANUFACTURER IN THE METROPLEX

Maxim Guillot, obviously a Frenchman, settled in Lancaster, Texas, where Preston Trail crossed Ten Mile Creek. He was wise enough to get near water and wood, because he planned to establish the first industry in the area, a foundry and a farm implement factory. He also made wagons. This industrious Frenchman, born in Angers, France, grew up in poverty. Finally, he was able to leave France, December 20, 1849. He arrived in New Orleans, February 1, 1850. First, Maxim worked for a gentleman who had a wagon business on Canal Street. He learned the business very quickly. However, when a yellow fever epidemic hit the town, the fine Frenchman decided to go to Shreveport. There he worked for a wagon factory and learned even more.

He stayed in Shreveport as long as he could, but his adventuresome nature could not be satisfied in this Northern Louisiana area. He needed more excitement. Guillot was always fascinated by the stories of the wild west. Everyone was interested in the wild west at that time. The stories of cowboys and Indians, gold mines and saloons with fancy ladies filled the minds of Easterners and Europeans. Some of these people were content living out these fantasies in their minds or in the reading of a dime novel. Guillot was not. He needed action, so he decided to fulfill some of his desires and go west.

Naturally, he made his own cart for the trip, using the wood from a sassafras tree. The whole wagon was made of wood. No nails were used — only wooden pegs finely crafted. This made the little cart extremely durable. Maxim got an old horse for nearly nothing and set out for the West — Denton County. Because he still did not speak English well, he had difficulties. At last, he met a Major Arnold, who could speak French. Maxim relied on Arnold to do some translating. Major Arnold, a very popular man around Denton County, was finally sent to Fort Worth. For some reason Guillot didn't follow his friend on westward but dropped down south a bit to Dallas. Without funds, he was forced to set up his wagon shop on the street. Very soon, however, the word got out that his wagons were well built and durable. He didn't have to advertise. People began to come to him from everywhere. Some came 350 miles to find this master wagon maker who was now known all over North Texas.

In 1853, Maxim Guillot went back to France to get himself a French wife. He may have loved the West, but none of the Texas girls were of his choosing. His mate had to be a French lady. He married and returned to the United States. This first wife did not live long, but she did bear him a son.

Monsieur Guillot was not only talented in the field of manufacturing, he was also very devoted to his church. In fact, in the summer of 1859, Rev. Fr. Sabastian Augagneur came to Dallas from Nacogdoches and read the first mass in the community in the home of Maxim Guillot. Later Father Augagneur went back to his native France to be a regimental chaplain in the French Army, but he returned later to Dallas and died here in 1869 in an epidemic of yellow fever.

In 1861, when the Civil War broke out, Guillot volunteered for the Confederate Army. However, because he was a master craftsman, he manufactured pistols and ammunition for the Texas Confederate troops. That site bears a historical marker — 220 W. Main, Lancaster, Texas, one block west of Dallas Avenue.

THE MEADOWS FOUNDATION

There is evidence all over our city that the Meadows Foundation is at work. This generous Meadows family has shared with almost every department of our city government. The Foundation has supported schools, businesses, and churches. They have restored, rebuilt, funded, and established culture centers, science centers, and arts centers. There is no end to what this family has done for this area. One of the latest additions to the city is the magnificent fence around Fair Park. This was given by the Meadows Foundation. On the SMU Campus, the arts building holds the Meadows Museum, which contains a fine collection of Spanish oil paintings. Mr. Algur Meadows declared that when he bought those paintings, it was the first time that he had ever put money into oil that was above the ground.

The Foundation is housed in a grand Victorian house on the

Wilson Block, 2900 Swiss. The houses situated on this block were built between 1899 and 1902 by Frederick and Henrietta Wilson. As the years passed, the neighborhood deteriorated and so did the houses. The Meadows Foundation restored them all and they are offered to non profit organizations for office space.

I had such a dear friend in Mrs. Lucille Meadows, a cute little lady who wore magnificent hats and drove a stretch limousine. She was so short that she could barely see over the steering wheel but she managed beautifully. Mrs. Meadows was the only member of First Baptist Church outside of Dr. Criswell himself who had her own parking space on Sundays.

In 1986, I was named Distinguished Alumna of the University of North Texas. The Meadows Foundation gives money to North Texas, so Mrs. Meadows called me. "This is Lucille. I want to go up and see you get that award. Fill my limo!" Well, since I was being declared distinquished and the distinguished Mrs. Meadows was giving me her limo for the evening, I thought that I had better fill it with distinguished people. I did! Rolling up to Denton in the Meadows limo was, of course, Mrs. Meadows, herslf. I selected as the driver a former student of mine, Benny Barrett, Dallas Police Officer. You couldn't want for a better driver. His wife Noni was in the group, of course. Then, there was my daughter Jill and her husband, Ken Beam. I invited Mrs. Fan Jones. Her husband, Dr. E. N. Jones, had been the president of Texas Tech. When he retired from Tech, he joined the consulting staff out at Dallas Baptist University. Mrs. Jones had been a Dean of Women and had married the president of the college. I always thought this was a great love match! My dear friend, Mary Frances Dent, an executive with Braniff, came along with another dear friend, Sue Herzog Johnson, who had been the private librarian for Everett DeGolyer. Now she is the law librarian for Carrington, Soleman, Sloman, and Blumenthal. We all had a terrific evening, thanks to Mrs. Meadows and her limo!

DOAK WALKER AND RUFUS C. BURLESON
STRANGE BEDFELLOWS

My good friend, Martha Albee, and I attended a Sunday School party at First Baptist Church. At the dinner, seated next to each other, were two great Dallasites, Mrs. Emma Cooper, 94 years old, and Dr. E. D. Walker, 94 years old. These two discussed everything that had ever taken place in Dallas for the past 94 years. In fact, Mrs. Cooper commented on what a delightful time she had. "I just loved talking with Dr. Walker. He knows everyone who's dead!"

The amazing thing about Dr. Walker is that he knows everyone who is dead and everyone who is alive too. He served as a teacher, principal, and administrator for the Dallas schools for years and years. Dr. Walker was in charge of hiring and firing the Dallas teachers, and to this day, he remembers everyone he hired and I guess he remembers those he fired too. Regardless, he loves to talk about his days with the DISD.

Dr. Walker is the father of Doak Walker, Highland Park football star, who contined to star at SMU, and later starred as a pro player. When Doak was initiated into the Football Hall of Fame just recently, as the father and son stood together, one could tell that there was a mutual admiration between them.

Mrs. Emma Cooper is the last living grandchild of Rufus C. Burleson, the great Baptist preacher who served as the first President of Baylor University when the school moved to Waco. There is a marvelous statue of Rufus on the Baylor campus that even the pigeons will not fly over, in deep reverence for this Baptist leader. Before Burleson went to Baylor, he was pastor of the First Baptist Church, Houston, Texas. He had two famous converts in his flock. One was Suzanna Dickenson, the lady of the Alamo, and the other was Sam Houston himself.

The Alamo heroes, William Travis, James Bowie, Davy Crockett, and James Bonham, were frontiersmen who had families, but those families were not at the Alamo. There was only one family man, Almeron Dickenson. He had a wife, Suzanna, and a baby, Angelina, living with him at the famous mission.

It became apparent to the men of the Alamo that they were going to be killed by the army of Santa Anna. William Travis drew the sword and drew the line on the ground. Everyone that was going to fight to the finish was to step on one side of the line. Those who were going to desert, were to go to the other side. Of course, everyone stayed to fight. James Bowie, who was ailing in his bed, had to be carried over the line. That scene is engraved into the heart of every Texan. Obviously, Almaron Dickenson joined the group that

118

was to fight to the end. He advised Suzanna to hide in the Baptistry. There was a possibility that she could survive there. Well, she did as her husband suggested, and she did survive. When the battle was over, she came out of the rubble. Santa Anna was startled, "If you'll leave in a hurry, I'll let you go," was the promise the Mexican General made to Mrs. Dickenson. She left in a hurry.

Suzanna probably hooked up with the frontiersman, Deaf Smith, and finally found her way to what was going to become Houston, Texas. When the city was founded by the great Sam, Mrs. Dickenson opened a boarding house. Actually, this house was more than a boarding house. To put it bluntly, Mrs. Dickenson offered more than room and board. Rufus Burleson was disturbed over this house. He went to Mrs. Dickenson. "Now, Mrs. Dickenson, the Lord loves you, but he doesn't like this house. Close it down and become a Baptist." She did! Later, when the little girl, Angelina, got married, Rev. Burleson performed the wedding ceremony.

Burleson's other great convert was Sam Houston. Sam had proven himself a hero in the War of 1812. He impressed General Andy Jackson so much that Andy began grooming Sam for the presidency of the United States. First, Houston served in the House of Representative from the State of Tennessee. Then, as planned, Sam was elected Governor of the State of Tennessee. All was progressing well politically, until Sam married. He married a girl who should have been thrilled to death to marry this six foot six, handsome leader. She stayed with Sam only a short time and left. Historians have never really decided upon the reason that she left him. Nevertheless, she was gone. Sam was devastated. He resigned as governor, became an alcoholic, and went to live with the Indians. Andy knew it was all over for Sam politically. "You're finished, Sam. You're a drunk. However, there's one thing you can do for me, and you can do it drunk. Go down to Texas, defeat the Mexican army, and bring Texas in as a state." Sam went to Texas. He defeated the Mexican army, but he didn't bring Texas into the union. He declared it a Republic and named himself President.

After serving as president for two years, Sam took a vacation to Alabama. There he met Margaret Lea, a beautiful Baptist girl. She was 18. He was 46. Her mother flipped over their courtship and came unglued when they married. Nevertheless, Margaret got Sam to quit drinking, and she made him attend the Baptist Church services. Finally, he was baptized into the Baptist faith by Rufus C. Burleson. Supposedly, Burleson dipped Sam into the river waters. "Your sins are washed away!" Sam Houston replied, "Then God help the fish." That story just might be true, but here's a Sam Houston baptism story that is true for sure. It's right from the lips of the granddaughter of Rufus C. Burleson. Mrs. Cooper said that when her grandfather dipped Sam into the water, he noticed that Sam still had his wallet in his back pocket. "I baptized you, Sam, but I also baptized your wallet. You're to tithe!" Sam always gave generously to the church.

THOSE EXCLUSIVE SCHOOLS FOR GIRLS

At the end of the 19th century, girls' schools were founded all over the country. Some were affiliated with churches, and some were privately owned and funded. Some were considered "finishing" schools and they "finished" girls right and left. Regardless, they were growing in number.

Father Joseph Mariniere, first pastor of the first Catholic parish in Dallas, Sacred Heart, in 1873, convinced the nuns from Galveston to come to Dallas and to open Ursuline Academy for girls. This first school for young ladies in Dallas is still very much in existence.

In 1889, Bishop Alexander C. Garrett, first Bishop of the newly formed Episcopal diocese, established St. Mary's College for girls. This school continued for some time, but it went by the wayside when Bishop Garrett could no longer give it his force and personality. Nevertheless, for the first decade of the 20th century, St. Mary's College became one of the places for discriminating parents to send their daughters.

In 1913, Miss Ela Hockaday established her school for girls in a gray framed house on Haskell Avenue where the old YWCA Boarding House still stands. She eventually moved the school in elegant quarters on the corner of Greenville and Belmont. Now, in elegant and massive quarters in far North Dallas the school thrives today.

There was a very exclusive girls' school established in Oak Cliff in 1888. It was called Oak Cliff College for Young Ladies. A gorgeous hotel was constructed in 1886 in Oak Cliff. The final cost was $100,000, and in those days that was a fortune. The hotel was beautifully furnished too. However, it fell into bankruptcy, so the ones holding the note were pleased to lease the magnificent structure to the school. The brochure advertising the college made this statement, "The building is heated by steam and thoroughly comfortable in winter and well ventilated in the summer."

Just before the school opened on September 7, 1888, a reception to welcome all the founders and faculty was given by Mrs. T. L. Marsalis. The newspaper reports that "the spacious and elegant dining hall was thrown open and twice filled by the visitors and iced confections and dainties were served by a trained corps of waiters." The school didn't last long, but it certainly had a classy beginning!

CLUB WOMAN, ADELLE TURNER —
CLUB HOUSES, ROSS AND ROSEMONT

One of the most dynamic and productive club women on the Dallas scene was Mrs. Adelle Turner. She married Edward P. Turner in 1879, and the couple decided to make Dallas their home. Mr. Turner gave his energies to his business and Adelle, Della to her friends, gave her energies to the organizing of women's clubs that would offer the ladies a lot of educational stimulation and many service opportunities.

On March 20, 1906, Mrs. Turner organized the Woman's Forum. She pointed out that it would be called a Forum, because the women would meet as the Romans did. The Roman Forum tried cases; the Woman's Forum would hold inspiring and thought provoking discussions and would present needy causes on which to act, and spiritual stirring endeavors on which to meditate. At every meeting there would be a mental, emotional, and spiritual challenge. There would be departments within the Forum — art, Bible, household economics, music, travel — just to name a few.

A club house was obtained — a two story frame house, 806 Akard. Eventually the Forum outgrew this house, and in 1930, under the financial guidance of Mrs. Turner, the ladies were able to buy the Alexander Mansion, 4607 Ross Avenue. Charles H. Alexander built this hugh house in 1906 for $125,000, quite extravagant for the time. There is a shower on the second floor that is worth taking the time to see. The knobs are descriptive of what part of the body a certain spout will squirt. In other words, one decides what spot of the body one wants sprayed, and by just turning knobs one can program a shower. There is a ballroom on the third floor, and the meeting rooms are on the second floor. The first floor has a magnificent dining room and library.

I have spoken many times to the members of the Dallas Woman's Forum, and I am always asked to wait in the library before ascending the stairs to address the ladies in their meeting room. The shelves of the library are filled with literary classics. Many of these books were given to the Forum by my former speech professor at the University of North Texas, Olive McClintic Johnson. She was head of the Speech and Drama Department when I was an undergraduate in 1949. An elegant woman, Mrs. Johnson spoke in a very elocutionary manner with all the proper gestures. "Please, students. You must project and enunciate!" she'd plead.

Mrs. Johnson did not have a Bachelor of Arts Degree, BA. She did not have a Bachelor of Science Degree, BS. She had a Bachelor of Oratory Degree, BO. We kids, of course, unknowing to her, always got tickled over her listing in the faculty directory. It read, "Olive McClintic Johnson, BO." Someone always pointed out, "Mrs. Johnson has BO!" Well, she did! Her oratorical training became obvious every time she opened her mouth to speak. How we loved her!

I'm filled with pride every time I give a program at the Forum and stand at the very podium Mrs. Johnson used. I'm not elegant, but I project and enunciate. Or as we say in the theatre, "I don't know how good I was, but I was loud."

With the Forum gaining members and prestige, Adelle Turner in 1926, organized another woman's club, the Oak Cliff Society of Fine Arts. These charming ladies today meet in a beautiful club house at 401 N. Rosemont. Mrs. Turner willed her home on Marsalis to the Fine Arts Society. When that house was razed for the construction of R. L. Thornton Freeway, the Society bought the house on Rosemeont for their meetings and socials.

That house was built by the Blake family. It was purchased later by Judge Ramsey and then later sold to Monta R. Ferguson, an attorney. The Ferguson family lived there for nine years. The house as well as Rosemont Street saw plenty of action, because the Fergusons had five very active girls. One daughter, Louise, told some very unusual stories.

A man came by the Ferguson home one day. He was "headin' West." He asked if he could spend the night but only on one condition. He had to tell how he "chased Johnny Reb." Well, the Fergusons were a family with deep Southern roots thus they refused to hear sories from this Yankee. They wouldn't let him stay.

The Ferguson family was one that did not indulge in worldly activities such as card playing. Louise remembered going over to the McHenry house across the street. This was where Uncle Mac, as he was fondly called, lived. McHenry built the Texas Theatre on Jefferson where Oswald, after the Kennedy assassination and the J. D. Tippit shooting, was captured. Uncle Mac was a big card player. Louise said she had to tiptoe around the room to avoid getting near a deck of cards that were always out on the table. These instruments of the devil did have to be avoided.

Colonel Daniel also lived on Rosemont. He was an unusual sort to say the least. But he gave marvelous parties for the kids in the neighborhood. They were served watermelon and buttermilk — just what any kid would want. He gave the kids trinkets which he said he had collected from his trips around the world. It was obvious that the little gifts came from Woolworth on Jefferson. The kids along with the Colonel pretended that they did come from places on the other side of the world. It was more fun that way. The Colonel's house had a tennis court and he kept a horse.

GEORGE KESSLER

President William Howard Taft visited Dallas in 1909. This was the year after the flood of 1908 that virtually devastated the city. Taft was honored at a banquet given at the Oriental Hotel. Those attending had to pay $25 a plate. This $25 was for the food only, since at that time there was a wave of "prohibition" sweeping the county. A dinner without alcohol was considered favorable.

The President came just when there was much talk about the Trinity River, since it had overflowed its banks the year before. This river could be a navigable waterway or it would be a menace to Dallas. It had overflowed its banks in what was certainly the most

123

damaging and almost the highest flood of its history. This set the city to once again thinking about the Kessler Plan. Kessler's plan would lead ultimately to the straightening of the river's channel and the erection of levees to make any such future flood an impossibility. But just who was this George Kessler and what was his plan?

As a lad, George Kessler, a poor widow's son, worked as a sack boy at the Sanger Brothers Store on Elm Street. He left Dallas and went north to Kansas City. There he did a fine job of planning the future of this Missouri town. Then he returned to work in Dallas. The city at that time was growing somewhat like Topsy. Dallas was growing fast, but without a plan. The city leaders were thrilled over the growth but very concerned about the placement of the growth. Thus, a plan was needed. Justin Kimball, Superintendent of Schools, wrote a book about the plan, *Our City, Dallas*. Kimball pointed out in his book that his father had noted many years before, "The trouble with Texas is that Texans cannot think out plans big enough to fit it." This was certainly true with the city of Dallas.

Kessler had foresight that one just couldn't believe. He put the control of the Trinity floods as Item I of his report. He told the citizens of Dallas, "The Trinity River project is the biggest problem you have today in Dallas. The building of levees in the Trinity River bottoms and the straightening of the river, extending from the mouth of Turtle Creek southward approximately three and one-half miles to four miles, would secure flood protection to the entire city. The filling of the new low lands outside and adjacent to these levees would provide additional room for railroad terminals and switching properties."

The city went with the plan and this project protected 3,336 acres of rich cotton land by building two levees in 1919, each levee 15 feet high. One levee protected the farms from the West Fork, and the other levee protected the farm land from Elm Fork. This proved to be the greatest and most far-reaching material step of progress ever yet undertaken in and for Dallas.

There were other items in the Kessler Plan.

2. Passenger and freight trains should be diverted from the residential streets of the city by belt lines around the city.

3. All passenger trains should be served by a Union Station. (This station was built as Kessler planned.)

4. The freight terminals of the railroads should all be put in the same part of the city. (This happened.)

5. A civic center as a worthy gateway to the city should be developed in front of the proposed Union Station.

6. As far as possible, grade crossings on streets and railroad tracks should be replaced by overpasses and underpasses.

7. Certain streets for traffic thoroughfares should be opened or broadened, especially across the business parts of the city.

8. A detailed plan was presented for the development of parks, parkways, boulevards, and playgrounds.

"There is not a single thing in this city that you need that you cannot do if you make up your mind that you need it and will have it; you will never establish a city under the feeling that you cannot do things."

George Kessler, 1911

"Taken all together, Mr. Kessler made probably the greatest single contribution to the future welfare of Dallas that has been made by any human being since John Neeley Bryan first built his little log cabin on the east bank of the Trinity."

Justin Ford Kimball, 1954

MR. SKILLERN

In 1965, when Skillern Drug Stores merged with Zale Corporation, wine and liquor bottles began to appear on the shelves of the stores. I can remember what my mother had to say about that. "Tsk, tsk! Mr. Skillern is rolling in his grave. He would never have allowed alcohol to be sold in his stores — such a staunch Methodist he was!" Mother knew Mr. Skillern when she was a child, and he was a man she could never forget.

The pioneer druggist, James Arthur Skillern, came to Dallas in 1896 and opened three drug stores. One was located at Commerce and Jefferson. This one was near the old Red Courthouse. (At that time, Jefferson Blvd. came on through to downtown.) Another store was located at 1812 Commerce, and the other one was opened in Oak Cliff. Later this first Oak Cliff store was sold, and Mr. Skillern acquired the Adolphus Pharmacy on Main Street.

Born in Tennessee in 1856, James Arthur Skillern graduated from Vanderbilt University with a degree in science. He always said that he learned not only to be a pharmacist, but also he learned honesty, perseverance and thrift, three virtues he displayed all of his life.

125

Skillern with a partner somehow found his way to Texas. The two druggists opened a store in Lewisville in 1875. In 1884, James married Mamie Edwards of Lewisville, whose family was originally from Georgia. Her father, Reverend Edwards, came to Texas in 1876 as a pioneer Methodist minister — circuit rider.

The store in Lewisville burned, so James decided to move his growing family to Sherman where he opened his own drug store in 1893. Eventually, the Skillern family would have nine children, so when James finally moved his family to Dallas, he had to find a big roomy house for his brood. He found one at 417 Ninth Street, Oak Cliff.

Everyone loved Mr. Skillern and his drug stores. This band of admirers, of course, included my mother. She remembered his big luxuriant handlebar mustache and his devotion to the Methodist church — good combination!

A report in the *Dallas Morning News* stated, "Each one of these establishments [the stores], because of the full line of quality goods, the dispatch of service rendered, and the Skillern personality, has popularized their locations until they are among the best known and patronized in Dallas."

Mr. James Arthur Skillern died in 1914. He was only 58 years old. His son, Frank Lloyd, took over until 1917, when another son, William Arthur, assumed the leadership of the business. In 1921, William Arthur suddenly died and another son, Rae E. Skillern, took over the business. This son led the stores into some really innovative actions. In 1935, he air conditioned the downtown store. This was really something! Then in 1944, the management announced that Skillern Drug Stores were getting ready for peacetime sales and service — whatever that meant! In 1954, the stores added some groceries and ready-to-wear to their inventory. Then in 1965, Skillern Drugs, after selling out, added wine and liquor to the stock. This was done much to the chagrin of my mother. In the early 1980s, Skillern Drug Stores disappeared, and the name Eckerd popped up all over the city.

ARMSTRONG MADE THE RIGHT MOVE

T. L. Marsalis and J. S. Armstrong were in partnership. In 1886, jointly, they owned some real estate and also a wholesale grocery business — strange combination. Shakespeare had better words

126

— "strange bed fellows." Nevertheless, the partnership was broken when T. L. Marsalis held an auction for some of their Oak Cliff lots. Marsalis decided that the lots were selling too quickly, so he engaged someone to bid on the lots so he could have them back. When Armstrong heard about this, he was shocked at the poor judgement of his partner. So, Armstrong came up with this ultimatum: "You take the real estate and I take the grocery buisness, or I take the real estate and you take the groceries. We are no longer partners." Marsalis took the Oak Cliff property and went broke trying to develop it. Actually, it wasn't the property itself that caused the loss. Oak Cliff property was very valuable. It was the panic of 1893, the depression, that brought down Marsalis.

In the meantime, Mr. Armstrong bought Colonel Exall's farm north of Dallas and in 1907 developed the first unit of Highland Park. Actually, it was Armstrong's sons-in-law, Edgar Flippen and Hugh Prather that did the developing. This area, Highland Park, became one of the most successful cities in America. Highland Park with the later developed, University Park, were never annexed into the city of Dallas. They've stayed separate and all must admit in their cases, the right move was made, monetarily speaking.

MARTIN WEISS

"I'm small, but I have energy like a steam roller on a downhill grade." This was the way Martin Weiss described himself. At the age of 13, he was running his family store in the little village of Vecs, nestled in the Carpathian Mountains in Hungary.

At the age of 20, he was a soldier like every other young man in his country. Bulgarian invasion was always a threat to Hungary, so military conscription was essential. He was wounded during a border skirmish (he had scars on his hands for life), and lying in the first-aid station, young Martin was given a choice — hospital or home. He chose home, of course.

While he was recovering, some friends visited and told of their grand trip to America. To the young Jewish lad, they seemed to be describing the promised land.

Young Martin decided he would somehow get to America, and he did. He worked, saved his money, and in the fall, 1887, he had enough to board a train in Budapest, tell his mother good-bye forever, and start the long trek to paradise.

127

On the ship coming over he worked as a dishwasher to acquire more needed cash. Then the magic moment arrived. Like so many immigrants of those times, he stood on the deck and saw the great lady in the harbor, the Statue of Liberty. Then, as part of the times, he was herded on to Ellis Island. Here's where deep loneliness set in, but Martin Weiss was determined to make it as a true American.

Like all immigrants, he felt that New York represented America. However, one day while working at a dollar a day job a man told him of a place where one could make six dollars a day — a fortune. Where was this place?

"It's Texas, boy! Texas! The biggest state in the country and a long way from here. It's the newest, fastest developing part of the United States."

In no time at all, Martin was in Gonzales, Texas. With his drive, determination, and knowledge he started as a peddler in this little South Texas town, went to San Marcos and acquired a store and a wife, and then got into a new deal in Beaumont. OIL!!! Unfortunately, a gigantic fire at Spindletop took all of his wells and he lost everything.

To satisfy his creditors, he had to sell his store in San Marcos. But he didn't waste time with regrets. He immediately put his mind to thinking of the next move.

Martin always appreciated good advertising. Seeing a Dallas paper one day, he noted that the big Dallas stores seemed to know how to advertise. So, in 1911, as a middle aged man starting all over, Martin and his family moved to Dallas. Through some former business contacts, he acquired a millinery supply business, and here in Dallas he made his company profitable for himself and the growing city.

In that little wicker furnished conference room in the back of the Weiss Building, 911 Elm Street, there was always a lot of action. Here, he promoted the Dallas Flying Club and the building of an air field between Dallas and Fort Worth. Here, he made certain there was a fine arts building at the Texas Centennial, 1936.

But, it was here, he did the greatest of all for Dallas. He was behind the building of the Triple Underpass and the new viaduct to the city on the other side of the Trinity. He was also behind the funding and the building of Methodist Hospital. All this progress was determined in a building that is still standing — one of the oldest buildings on Elm Street.

BILL McCRAW, DISTRICT ATTORNEY

"Bristol Myers, makers of Ipana for the Smile of Beauty and Sal Hepatica for the Smile of Health, brings you Mr. District Attorney — champion of the people — defender of truth — guardian of our fundamental rights to life, liberty, and the pursuit of happiness." Remember that old radio show that had its debut in 1939? That show played on Wednesday nights for years bringing to the listening audiences exciting adventures from the DA's office. Dallas had a very wild and woolly, rip-roaring, sensational DA in the 20s. His name was Bill McCraw, and some of his activities made national headlines.

Bill first served as an assistant district attorney, and this is when he first became nationally known. The year was 1925. The month — November. Bill McCraw was arguing a case in the court of Judge Felix Robertson. Judge Robertson, a very mild mannered man, threw out the arson case. Bill McCraw, with red hair and hot temper, sassed the judge for his decision. The usually laid back judge, roused by the back talk, sentenced Bill McCraw to three hours in jail for contempt of court. Bill, still hot under the collar, yelled back, "Why not make it three months? I hear the food is good." The judge, now red in the face, bellowed, "Three days in the county jail!" He then rapped the gavel, thus sealing the pronouncement.

Arrangements were made for Bill to serve his three days between his cases. However, because he was too busy to ever have time off, it was decided that Bill McCraw would go to jail over the weekend. This did not suit him at all, because Bill taught the Boethian Sunday School class at Cliff Temple Baptist Church. Still there was nothing else he could do. He went to jail on Saturday, and on Sunday morning, his Sunday School class, 150 members, went to the county jail for their lesson. They figured that if their teacher couldn't come to them, they could go to the teacher. Bill McCraw stood behind bars and taught the lesson to his students on the outside. The lesson dealt with Paul before Agrippa. This story made the papers all over the country.

Bill McCraw became district attorney in 1926. Later he was elected Attorney General of Texas, and in 1938, he ran for Governor of the state. That was a bad year for anyone to run for Governor of Texas, because really no one had a chance to win over W. Lee O'-

Daniel. The state worshipped O'Daniel. Bill McCraw had to admit that his own mother said, "Son, I can't vote for you. I have been an O'Daniel fan for years. He's a good man. He has my vote."

In 1941, the United States went to war. Bill had served in World War I and now he was once again ready to go. The army said he was too old. He protested! When he was declared physically perfect, Bill left to serve as the only Colonel with a sea command in the army. He was anchored on the steam ship, Rebecca Lukens, at Okinawa and also at Saipan. The ship was in these strategic spots to repair fighter planes.

After the war in 1954, Governor Allen Shivers appointed Bill McCraw as judge of the newly formed 3rd District Court. He was known as "99 Years McCraw" because of his stiff sentences.

Bill had a varied career. He did some writing and editing for the *Baptist Standard.* He was always in demand as an after dinner speaker. He wrote a book on politicians. He was going strong when at the age of 59, he died suddenly of a heart attack.

BISCUITS AND GRAVEYARDS

If you grew up in Texas during the 1930s like I did, you stopped dead in your tracks everyday at noon. No one moved a muscle when the clock struck twelve except to reach over and turn on the radio. "WBAP, Fort Worth, Texas. In cooperation with Burrus Mills, makers of Light Crust Flour and other fine baking products, the Light Crust Doughboys are on the air." There would be this twang from one string of a guitar, and then the Doughboys would start to sing.

> "Never do brag, never do boast, we sing our songs from coast to
>   coast,
> We're the Light Crust Doughboys from Burrus Mills. Listen
>   everybody near and far, if you want to know who we are,
> We're the Light Crust Doughboys from Burrus Mills. If we're
>   ever out your way, we'll come in and spend the day,
> We're the Light Crust Doughboys from Burrus Mills."

Then the announcer would introduce W. Lee O'Daniel, founder and leader of the group.

Willard Lee O'Daniel came to Forth Worth in 1925, as sales manager for Burrus Mills. He had to sell Light Crust Flour, so he

130

organized a country band known as the Light Crust Doughboys to do just that — sell flour. The musicians made $7.50 a week, but they also had to work at the mill. The Doughboys played for years, and fortunately, for the metroplex area they're still playing. One of the original members, Smokey Montgomery, is a good buddy of mine and he still strums a mean banjo. Nevertheless, Willard Lee (We Texans love double names — Lonnie Roy, Billy Bob, Sue Ellen, etc.) became so popular with the people of Texas, that he decided to run for governor of the state. Of course, when he campaigned, he took the Doughboys with him. They played; he spoke. W. Lee called himself, "Pappy" O'Daniel, and the then well known phrase, "Pass the biscuits, Pappy," which came from selling flour, was shouted at all the political rallies. O'Daniel won the election.

Pappy O'Daniel did not stop with the governorship. He ran for the U.S. Senate in 1941. The Doughboys went up to Washington. In that senate race, O'Daniel defeated a man who said he would never be defeated in Texas again. "I was beaten by those Doughboys, but I'll never lose again."

After O'Daniel, Texas had a great governor, Coke Stevenson. After serving as governor, he too decided to run for the U.S. Senate against that man who said he'd never lose again. This race was the closest race in Texas history. On September 2, 1948, Stevenson was 249 votes ahead with 253 of the 254 counties reporting. It looked like he had defeated that man who vowed never to be defeated again. This man was so mad that he went down to his henchman in South Texas, George Parr. "George, I've lost." George was quick to answer. "Now, Lyndon, you haven't lost, because we haven't voted yet in South Texas. This was eleven days after the election. So the Jim Wells County men under Parr all went out to the graveyard to vote. Suddenly, from Box 13, 202 votes came in for Johnson and 1 lone vote was cast for Stevenson. Texas history school books usually read, "By 87 questionable votes, from Box 13, Lyndon Johnson won the senate race." The rest, you can assuredly say, is history.

Several jokes came out of that election. "Maria, why are you crying?" "Oh, Grandpa came back from the dead last night to vote but didn't come by to see us." It was said that one name on a tomb stone was very long and very hard to spell. The tomb stone voter decided to skip that grave. His partner said, "No, write it down. He has just as much right to vote as anyone else."

131

When I was teaching at Dallas Baptist University during the Johnson years, I'd tell this story to my classes. The kids were always worried about my being carted off to the Federal Penitentiary for slander. I assured them that the story had been published many times. Everyone knew about those votes. Incidentally, the kids of the 60s didn't like Lyndon Johnson because of the war. If the guys didn't make their grades, they had to go to Vietnam.

One day, a man came into my classroom with his brief case chained to his wrist — pretty official looking. He needed to see me. The kids really thought that this was it. I was leaving for prison. It turned out that the man was just investigating a former student who had applied to work for the CIA. I returned to the classroom and began lecturing. The class interrupted. "Well, will you be jailed?" I smiled. "Heavens no! No one goes to jail for telling about Lyndon. It's all true!"

Actually, this story has another personal ending to it. When my husband, Jack, got out of the service in 1955, he became the junior high band director in Alice, Texas. Alice is the County seat of Jim Wills County, Box 13. There we were — right in the middle of Parr country.

Since I had a degree in drama, and since I certainly did not want my marvelous dramatic ability to go to waste, I organized the Alice Little Theatre. Immediately, I found out that there was a shortage of leading men in Alice, Texas. Not knowing what else to do, I coerced my husband to take a leading role in the play. He didn't have time to really learn his lines, but he went on anyway. Opening night, Mr. and Mrs. George Parr with Parr's CPA and his wife were in the audience. One of the ladies drank just a tad too much and fell out of her chair in the middle of my husband's big scene. Jack totally forgot not only his lines but also the entire play. The woman was carried out by the others in the party — wrists and ankles held, and Jack vowed never to appear on the stage in a play again. I always said that George Parr created Lyndon Johnson's political future, but he ruined Jack Rumbley's dramatic career.

HOLLAND'S MAGAZINE

Dr. Imogene Bentley Dickey Mohat is one of the most inspiring people I have ever met. Dr. Mohat was the Dean of Women at the University of North Texas when I went there as an undergrad-

132

uate in 1949. She was stern, but she was fair. We girls were all afraid of her, and naturally, we called her the "Mean Dean" or "Big Red," because of her flaming red hair. Nevertheless, I was impressed by this lady, because she knew so much. As an undergraduate, I decided that I'd try to follow in her footsteps. She held a Ph.D., so in the back of my mind I always had this desire to acquire a doctorate. Eventually, I got this degree. It took me ten years, but I did it. A great moment in my life, the icing on the cake, so to speak, came when my doctoral dissertation was published. I had written about the Dallas schools, so on the 100th anniversary of public education in Dallas, my book, *A Century of Class*, Eakin Press, was published.

Dr. Mohat also got the icing on the cake, in that her dissertation was published as very interesting reading, *Early Literary Magazines of Texas*. In her book, she has a chapter on a magazine that was published in Dallas for 48 years — *Holland's Magazine, the Magazine of the South*. This magazine arrived every month at our house for years, and every month when it came, my mother would say, "Oh, good. *Holland's* has arrived. I lived next door to the Hollands. Mrs. Holland was such a beautiful woman."

Frank P. Holland published a magazine, *Farm and Ranch*, beginning in 1883. His son, Frank P. Holland, Jr., joined his father in 1900 and decided that there should be a magazine that would serve all of the people of the South and Southwest — not just the farm and ranch crowd. Frank Jr. bought out *Street's Weekly* and began to publish *Holland's*. He promised the subscribers of *Street's Weekly* a good deal. *Holland's* was offered for $1 a year. *Street's Weekly* was $2 a year. If all the readers of *Street's* would keep up their subscriptions, they would save a dollar. These readers were promised great fiction. This pledge was printed in the August 1905 issue. "Each month there will be a number of strong stories, full of life and action, yet pure and clean — stories that can be read by the fireside and enjoyed in the home by each member of the family."

There were other sections: floriculture, fashion's frills, culinary affairs, and cosmetic economy to name a few. The magazine itself was not the size of a standard magazine. It was much larger — like the weekend guide in the newspaper. It wasn't very thick, but it was full of great stories. That I remember.

We subscribed to *Holland's Magazine* until the end of its publication, December 1953. As I said, I remember the stories. I don't know if they were pure and clean. I don't believe that we ever read them at our family fireside. But I do remember that every month when the magazine arrived my mother would say, "Oh, good. *Holland's* has arrived. I lived next doore to the Hollands. Mrs. Holland was such a beautiful woman."

WILLIAM COOMBS

The Coombs family came to the colonies long before the family of George Washington arrived. Like the Washington family, the Coombs family, Joseph and Matilda, came to Virginia from England. After Joseph and Matilda, there were John and Alice Jolly Coombs. Their son, William Nelson and Hanna Gloves Coombs, had little Zachariah, who was only ten years old when his family came to Texas in 1843. Actually, there were three Coombs boys that came to Texas. They acquired land through the Peters Colony contract. William Coombs was the first person to build a "plank" house west of the Trinity. All the other houses were log cabins. William claimed the land that would lie in the area from Beckley and Zang to Davis. Issac Coombs claimed the land that would lie east of Hampton and Davis to the old Jim Town. L. G. Coombs lived in the Cement City area.

William, a first Grand Master in Masonry in Texas, served as Chief Justice of Dallas County. As he grew older he told grand stories of how during Reconstruction days after the Civil War, he tried his best to endure the Yankees.

Son Zachariah became a preacher and a judge. Wouldn't you expect that with a name like Zachariah? His full name was Zachariah Ellis Coombs. He was a scholar, a lawyer, teacher, preacher, legislator, judge, Confederate soldier, husband, and father. Zachariah preached for a while at the Western Heights Church of Christ, 1912 N. Winnetka. This church was founded in 1872, and it's still holding services. The first day that Zachariah preached, there were 50 converts. They were baptized in the creek that is now named after the family — Coombs Creek. It was so cold on that day that the ice had to be broken in order to immerse the converts. Coombs

Creek flows around and through Stevens Park Golf Course, follows I-30, twists a bit, and flows right into the Trinity on the south side of the I-30 bridge.

IN THE SERVICE OF . . .

When Buckner Benevolences was 100 years old in 1979, I was asked to produce a play depicting Father Buckner's founding of the orphan's home. The cast would be made up of the children that were then out at Buckners. When I was a kid and Daddy would drive by Buckner Orphans Home, I would cry, because those kids didn't have a nice mother and father like I did. Daddy always assured me that they were well taken care of. They were happy. Today, the children are not orphans. They are abused and neglected kids, but the staff at Buckners opens it arms to these children and are working diligently to help these kids become emotionally stable adults. The arms of Buckner now extend to the older citizens. A retirement village and nursing home are part of the vast Buckner facility. It has come a long way since Robert Cooke Buckner took in stray, needy kids. His heart was so moved when one evening a little boy knocked on his door. "Would you take me in? I can pay you!" And the child extended his hand that held a couple of pennies. Dr. Buckner, beloved Baptist preacher, wept soundly. He decided then and there he'd get the money together to open the orphan's home.

Everyone in that large Buckner family has contributed to the world. The departed members are all buried out at Grove Hill Cemetery across the street from my parents. When I visit Mother and Daddy, I always go across the street and say "Hi!" to the Buckners. They not only have head stones on the graves, but they also have foot stones. Don't start this tradition at your family plot unless you're like the Buckners who have all done something. Those foot stones read — Mother, Father, Doctor, Missionary, Pastor, Nurse, etc. No foot stone reads — Black Sheep, or even worse is blank. Can you imagine a blank — he did nothing. No problem with the Buckers. They all contributed. They all served, and they're still serving. They served the Lord and Dallas, Texas.

Within the Disciples of Christ Church there is a similar story of charity. Mr. Peak, a wealthy man who developed East Dallas and named the streets after his boys — Carroll, Junius, Worth, Victor, etc. — also had daughters. One was Juliette, a beautiful girl who was chosen the first May Queen of Dallas, 1858. That year she married a promising young attorney, A. Y. Fowler. The young couple moved to Fort Worth where Mr. Fowler joined with another attorney, John Peter Smith. The Fowlers had a beautiful baby, but when the child was nine months old, it died. Juliette was expecting a second child when her husband was brutally murdered. When her baby was born it lived only a short time. The beautiful May queen who was to live happily ever after, suddenly had no one. She moved back to Dallas to live with her parents. Juliette never remarried but instead gave her life to the welfare of others. She had this dream of a home for needy children and older adults. Often she took the needy into the Fowler mansion on Peak and Worth, all the while working to establish a properly certified institution. Before the dream was completed, she died in 1889 at the age of 52. However, her will provided the funds for the Juliette Fowler Home. Her sister, Sarah Harwood, made certain all was done as her sister wished. To this day, the Juliette Fowler Home provides help for children and offers residences for older adults.

FAIR WEATHER AND FINE MUSIC:
THE CLINES

We wake up in the morning, look out of the window, and determine the weather condition for the day. If our own predictions don't satisfy us, we turn to the trusty weathermen. Today, we have quite an assembly of these forecasters. However, in 1901, the Dallas Weather Bureau started with one man, Dr. Joseph Cline. Dr. Cline graduated from a college in Tennessee and later joined his brother in Galveston, Texas. There he began work for the weather bureau. In 1900, he predicted the Galveston hurricane that swept the island, September 8, killing almost 8,000 people. In those days, even if the path and force of the hurricane were known, there was little anyone could do. Thousands were injured and the damage amounted to 17 million dollars. Dr. Cline told his whole story in a book, *When the Heavens Frowned*. Through the tempest he was able to save some children, but so many more were lost. Because Dr. Cline accurately predicted this hurricane, he was sent to the U.S. Weather Bureau in Puerto Rico. Later he was sent to Corpus Christi, and from Corpus he moved to Dallas.

The first weather bureau was in the old Cotton Exchange building on Akard Street. It was later moved to the new exchange on St. Paul Street, and then it was consolidated with the Love Field Airway Service.

Dr. and Mrs. Cline reared a son, Durward Cline, musician. "Mama" Cline never considered music a proper field, so to satisfy "Mama" and his musical talent, Durward opened a music store at 1107 Elm Street. That store was the headquarters for band students of the area. Also piano students bought their music there. I have many piano solos with "Cline Music" stamped on the front. I also have several little glass and wooden pianos that were given to me by my piano teacher for fine practicing. On the bottoms of the relics still cling labels reading "Cline Music."

Durward had the business, but regardless of "Mama" he also had a dance band. Actually, he organized it while he was a student at Oak Cliff High. Durward Cline and his band were known all over the region. It was a great group, because my husband, Jack, said that it was. Jack played many a "gig" with Durward.

There was something else very unusual about Durward Cline. He had a distinctive way of expressing himself. His speech had a definite flair. It was sprinkled with what fellow musicians called "Clinisms." In Oxford, England, a professor, Dr. William Archibald Spooner, was known for transposing sounds. These transpositions were known as Spoonerisms. Witty and unwitting transpositions of sound were also part of Durward Cline's speech. In other words, he transposed more than the tunes his band played. He'd shift into these verbal gems.

In referring to his car: "I just bought four good New Year tires."

In referring to the actions of others: "That guy wouldn't give half a man a chance." "That fellow follows me around like I was a puppy dog." "He watched me like I was a hawk."

Describing his wife's Christmas present: "I gave her a new A.M.-P.M. radio."

If things didn't go as he wished, he's say: "Had I wanted a fool to do it, I would have done it myself."

About the band business: "The economy is so bad I can't book anything but a five or six piece trio job."

To the band: "Leave early, so if we're late, we'll be on time."

To the band going out of town: "Watch it in Seagoville. They're giving all the policemen tickets."

Referring to a girl singer: "She's no fried chicken." To the band when HE was late: "I was late because I got in front of a big truck and couldn't get around it."

When he got lost on the way to a job, he asked for directions. Rolling down the car window he shouted: "Is this the road we're on?"

Glen Miller died years ago, yet his band played on. Durward, in thinking of the band asked: "What's the name of that band that the guy that died is running?"

To the band: "It's a western party. Wear a white sleeved shirt with a banana around your neck."

When a band member said he couldn't hear an announcement, Durward responded: "Turn your stand light on."

Durward sired two sons, Jack and Jerry, who ran the music store for a while and also played in the band. They are proud of their talented and illustrious father and grandfather. Were Durward Cline alive today and were he to read this essay, he'd appreciate every word. After all, a good hand is always worth more than a bush.

TAKE ME OUT TO THE BALL GAME

When Nolan Ryan steps up to pitch for the Texas Rangers at Arlington Stadium, a million dollar complex which will soon be overshadowed by a multimillion dollar compound, he represents great baseball in the Metroplex today. However, behind Ryan and the Rangers, in those thrilling days of yesteryear, baseball had some very humble but interesting beginnings in Dallas.

The stadium was called Burnett Field where the Dallas Eagles played, but actually, in the very beginning, it was Rebel Stadium where the Dallas Rebels played.

The original stadium was built on the lower end of Jefferson Blvd. in 1925. Long before on that same spot was Gardner Park with its indoor swimming pool. Later the pool was converted into an ice skating rink. This building burned in August 1924, and the baseball stadium was built the next year. Unfortunately, it was made of wood, so fire claimed this structure in September, 1940. A new stadium was ready in April 1941. It opened in spite of the fact that the bleachers were not constructed. Of course, they were completed soon after with additional seats which made the seating capacity stand at 10,600. Owing to wartime material shortages, this stadium was roofless until 1946.

This time was the heyday — the golden times of the minors. Among the club owners were men who left an indelible imprint on the Dallas scene: J. Walter Morris, George Schepps, R. W. (Dick) Burnett, J. W. Bateson, Amon Carter, Jr., Ray Johnston, Tommy Mercer, and later, Lamar Hunt. Except for the multiple changes in ownership, particularly in the late years, and an occasional face lifting, for thirty years the stadium defied time and change. However, in the 1960s it became a crumbling mass. Today, there's nothing on the spot but memories.

There was a great night in 1946 when the stadium couldn't hold all the fans. Part of the crowd overflowed onto the field and almost encircled the park. That night the Eagles scored a 5 to 1 victory over the Atlanta Crackers. For all the old fans, here's the way George White, then sports editor of the *Dallas Morning News* described the victory.

> Borom beats out a swinging bunt to second baseman Charlie Glock to start the rally. Pitcher Tom Pullig's sacrifice down the first base line moves Borom to second, and Gene Markland's single to center scores him with the tying run. Markland went to second on the throw home. An intentional walk to Al Carr, Clint Conatser's single past short, Bob Moyer's infield hit to the left of the box, a walk to Hal Hirshon and Red Davis' single through the middle, rounded out the rally.

These guys are long gone, but baseball stays with us forever. Besides the game, there was added entertainment — Miss Inez Teddlie at the organ. Miss Inez kept a well thumbed notebook filled with song titles on the music stand. From her seat behind home plate, Inez kept a close watch on the proceedings so that she could co-ordinate her music with the game. Actually, she knew a lot about baseball!

When the deep reaches of the outfield ever got flooded, she would burst out with "Cruising Down the River." When the game would drag into the eleventh inning, she delivered "It's Been a Long, Long Time." The Dallas Eagles' theme song was "Under the

139

Double Eagle March." Inez would swing out with that march when the umpires walked on the field. She also played the march during the seventh inning stretch. When the Eagles themselves ran out on the field, strands of "Take Me Out to the Ball Game" could be heard all over Oak Cliff and Downtown Dallas. Fans walked out of the stadium to the same tune. If a pitcher got sour with his curves and had to be removed from the context, Inez tootled, "April Showers." Home-run hitters trotted around the bases to the tune of "Waitin' for the Robert E. Lee." Miss Inez chose that number because the opening words, "Way over the levee," sounded apropriate for the moment. If the Eagles were losing, the organ played softly, "Look for the Silver Lining."

One evening, May 21, 1949, to be exact, an added attraction arrived in the form of Wee Bonnie Baker, the singer. She rose to fame with her song, "Oh, Johnny," which she included in her repertoire before the Burnett fans that evening. Stars like Bonnie Baker traveled around in those days and appeared wherever there was a crowd. The week before, Eddie Bracken, the comedian, had appeared at the game. These stars would perform and then go up into the press box to be interviewed on radio. Announcer Jerry Doggett was always on hand for all the excitement.

NANCY REAGAN WAS WRONG!

When the Reagans left the White House, Nancy went home to California and wrote her book, *My Turn.* Concerning her mother's acting career, she wrote, "Mother gave up her career when she got married, but she didn't stop working. Chicago was the capital of the radio soap operas and mother continued working on radio, because she could do voices and dialects." Mrs. Reagan pointed out that her mother could do the black accent very well. Because of this, she worked on a soap opera entitled, *Betty and Bob.* After this her mother joined *Amos and Andy.* "Mother was the only woman to appear on the *Amos and Andy Show.*" Nancy, you are WRONG!!!!

There was a charming lady by the name of Madaline Basford who grew up in Oak Cliff that appeared on the *Amos and Andy Show.* Madaline studied elocution, expression and dramatic arts and was always giving readings at Cliff Temple Baptist Church for socials and programs. Since Madaline was so successful at Cliff Tem-

140

ple Baptist, she decided to try New York/Chicago, the entertainment capitols of the nation. She landed a part on the *Amos and Andy Show*. She was Miss Blue. Andy had a famous and familiar phrase on the show, "Buzz me, Miss Blue." Well, Madaline Basford was Miss Blue.

Magaret Bassett Johnson, whose father was Dr. Bassett, pastor of Cliff Temple, was in New York just starting her show biz career, when Madaline landed the Miss Blue role on radio. Margaret's first daughter was born a little later on, and to this day that daughter is called "Miss Blue" in honor of Madaline's part.

Nancy Reagan's mother was not the only woman on the *Amos and Andy Show*. There was Madaline Basford from Dallas!

THE FRONT PORCH, THE BLUE GOOSE, AND THE MOON MAIDS — THEY ALL SORT OF GO TOGETHER

When I was a kid and the temperature got up into the 90s and the 100s, we all immediately went to the front porch. It was the only cool place around. We sat in those rounded metal chairs that were so popular before World War II. Skillern's Drug store sold them for 99¢. They came in green, red, yellow, and blue. They were so sturdy and uncomfortable, that they lasted forever. I still have two of the old relics out on my patio. They have at least 36 coats of paint on them. I don't think anyone or anything could ever destroy them.

Nevertheless, we'd all sit out on the porch in those stiff chairs and fan with the newspaper or with one of those well remembered funeral parlor fans. If the funeral parlor didn't give those fans out, someone running for office would see that every voter would have one. I remember one with "Keep Cool With Pool" on it. This was when Joe Pool was first running for public office. My mother had one of those fold-out oriental fans that she kept handy for porch sitting.

When the temperature got up to 104 degrees during the afternoons, my mother and I had a simple way of cooling down. I'd go up to Mr. Finley's drug store and buy a pint of ice cream for 15¢, two Cokes for a dime, and the latest copy of *The Woman's Home Companion*. We drank Coke floats and read stories from the magazine.

Mr. Finley's drug store was on the corner of Greenville and Goodwin, where the Blue Goose Restaurant is now located. I walk into the Blue Goose today, look down at that terrazzo flooring, and remember when Mr. Finley put that floor in his store. We kids all read comic books where the Blue Goose bar is now. We couldn't afford to buy the books, so Mr. Finley, with all his kindness, allowed us to read them free of charge. We did have to put them back on the shelf in good condition. After all, he was in business.

All the men who owned stores in that section of shopping on Greenville were nice. Mr. Flannagan had the school supply store where Stans Blue Note is now located. Mr. Stites Garage was in the now defunct theatre next to Stans. He was so nice. If the repair bill on your car was a little much, he would arrange for you to pay it off in convenient amounts. On the west side farthest south, was Mr. Thomas's cleaners. He was a nice guy. They all were — Mr. Finley, Mr. Flannagan, Mr. Stites, and Mr. Thomas — to name a few.

Well, nevertheless, the front porch days of coke floats are gone. In the first place, there are no front porches around. Most of them have been glassed in and have air conditioners hanging out of one of the windows. New homes never had front porches in the first place.

Now, in the thrilling days of yesteryear, one of the grandest front porches in Dallas was on the Grogan house. This rambling home sat on the bluff at the corner of Fort Worth Avenue and Sylvan. Mrs. Grogan's father, Samuel Dickey Bradley after a very active life, retired to that porch. He would tilt his chair back on the railing and view the land, philosophize a bit, and chat with a group of pretty classy people who would drop by occasionally and join him on the porch.

Before his time on the front porch Grandpa Bradley owned a feed store on College Avenue near Baylor Hospital. He was a grand public servant, giving much of his time to the levee committee. He was also involved with the founding of the Western Heights Church of Christ, and he also was part of the West Dallas School Board. West Dallas High, located on Walmsley Street, was just down the street from the big house. Sidney Lanier Elementary School stands on that site now. When the old school was torn down, Grandpa's name was on the cornerstone.

The list of people who joined Grandpa Bradley on that front porch reads like Who's Who in Dallas. Judge J. A. Crawford was a regular. Justin Kimball, Superintendent of Schools, would drop by and sit a spell. George Kessler, himself, was part of the porch crew, and Judge Zechariah Ellis Coombs tilted his chair and enjoyed the view. Judge W. H. Hord's daughter sometimes walked by in her elegant dresses and waved to the whole gang.

The next time you're on Interstate 30 going to Fort Worth, look up just before the Hampton exit. You'll see this beautiful bluff where once stood the Grogan house. There's an old crumbling tourist court there now.

The Grogan porch is gone, but the Grogans are still stirring. They don't sit on front porches. My friend, Ruth Grogan, is quite an active lady today. Harrold Grogan, her brother, is performing all over the place.

When my husband and I were at the University of North Texas, we knew Mary Jo Thomas, Tinker Cunningham, and Harrold Grogan. They were all great vocalists. Mary Jo and Tinker were wisked off to fame by Vaughn Monroe. He was looking for a back up vocal group and these two ladies from North Texas were in a group that Vaughn Monroe heard, liked and took. He called them the Moon Maids, and they toured the world singing with Vaughn. Finally, when music styles began to change and close harmony groups were not as popular, the girls returned to Dallas. Mary Jo married Harrold Grogan and Tinker married William Rautenberg. Today, the girls are back together again. They recruited June Branton from Arlington and Carol Piper from Dallas to sing with them. Carol's husband, Bob Piper, was a composer/artist with Tom Merriman, TM Productions, for years. Bob writes the vocal arrangements for the group. They bill themselves now as The Moon Maids Plus One. Harold Grogan is the Plus One.

BONNIE AND CLYDE

Nowadays, just anybody can be a criminal. All you have to do is commit a crime. This wasn't true in the 1930s. Criminals then had personality and individuality which brought on notoriety and prestige. They were known! Take Bonnie and Clyde, for instance, who were certainly well known in the Dallas area. My mother and

143

father had friends that got married in 1933. As the happy couple was leaving the reception, one of the guests exlaimed, "My Word! They look like Bonnie and Clyde." The bride and groom almost didn't leave. They were afraid of being apprehended by the police, who were definitely keeping a sharp eye out for the two outlaws. Actually, saying that the couple looked like Bonnie and Clyde really wasn't very complimentary. Bonnie and Clyde did not look like Warren Beatty and Faye Dunaway. The real bandits were ugly — especially Bonnie.

Clyde Barrow was born November 24, 1909, Talico, Texas. His father was a tenant farmer who tried desperately to support the family which consisted of eight children. Eventually, he moved his family to Dallas, where he bought a combination house and filling station at 1221 Singleton Blvd. The building is still there, but it is not occupied at this time. Barrow sold the property in 1940 to a man named Willis for $800. In the 1970s it was a tortilla factory.

Clyde was a typical kid — always searching for a way to make some money. For a while he worked with his friend, Charles "Chili" Blatney, at Blatney's father's mirror shop on Swiss Avenue. The boys were always checking for money that could have possibly been stashed behind a mirror that was brought in to be resilvered. Chili remembered that Clyde always wore a funny hat which he was quick to remove and to beat on the floor in merriment when he'd get tickled over a joke that was told. The Blatneys were always there to give a hand to the poor, struggling Clyde.

Later Clyde worked in a soap factory. It was here that he took out a life insurance policy on himself. He was careful to keep up the payments on it even when he was on the run. He paid 20¢ a week on that policy which did pay his mother $820 when Clyde was gunned down by Texas Ranger, Frank Hamer, on May 23, 1934.

Bonnie Parker was born on October 1, 1910, in Rowena, Texas, Runnels County. Her parents were divorced and eventually she made her way to Dallas where she lived just off Lamar Street, where Sears is today. Bonnie first worked as a waitress in a cafe near the Court House. Then she went to work for Clyde's sister who owned a beauty shop. This is where she met Clyde. He was out of prison at the time on a "Ma Ferguson" pardon.

After the two met and began their spree of robberies and murders, they both stayed close to the Barrow family. They'd drive into the little filling station and leave notes in empty Coke bottles. They also informed the family that they had buried some money on a small street just off Abrams Road. The Barrow family is still looking for that loot today.

Many felt sorry for Clyde. They claimed he was actually a very talented person — just misdirected. He had a beautiful baritone voice and he played the saxophone quite well. Many a friend vouched for the fact that he belonged in a big band — not on the road to crime. Clyde was also a great driver. He could have been an A. J. Foyt if given the chance. He could really maneuver a Ford. However, he was always quick to give the credit for the good maneuvering to the car itself. In 1934, just one month before he was gunned down, he wrote Henry Ford a letter. "Dear Sir: While I still got breath in my lungs I will tell you what a dandy car you make. I have drove Fords exclusively when I can get away with one. The Ford V-8 has got other cars skinned. Even if my business hasn't been strictly legal it don't hurt anything to tell you what a fine car you make in the V-8."

Clyde Barrow is buried in the Western Heights Cemetery, 1617 Ft. Worth Avenue. There is a big sign posted — NO TRESPASSING! The tomb stone has been stolen many times. It reads — *Clyde Barrow. Gone but not forgotten.*

Bonnie Parker is buried at Crown Hill Cemetery on Webbs Chapel Road. Her family had the tomb stone so grounded that it has never been stolen. It reads — *Bonnie Parker. As the flowers are made sweeter by the sunshine and dew so this old world is made brighter by the lives of folks like you.*

DAGGER PREWITT

There were other notorious, 1930s style killers in Dallas. One was Dagger Prewitt. His victims were drivers stopping for red lights. Dagger would rush out from nowhere, open the car door, and thrust a dagger into the unsuspecting prey. Naturally, people kept their car doors locked, but sometimes a person would forget. This killer left the daggers in his victims — thus the name — Dagger.

My father got to see 'ole Dagger after he was captured and placed in prison. At that time, if one served on the jury he was priv-

145

ileged to go through the jail and look at the prisoners. This was an added reward given for jury duty, if you can call it a reward. Dagger had the reputation of being the best dressed man in jail. My daddy was serving on the jury and got to see the natty and dapper Mr. Prewitt.

When my father saw this killer, the memory of a dark and dreary night came to daddy's mind. "It was a real robber's night," my father remembered. Daddy always called rainy nights, robber's nights. Because of this description, I have never liked rainy nights. Well, anyway, it was one of those nights. Daddy was coming home from work and stopped by the grocery store for a few items. He came out of the store, got into the car, and placed the sack of groceries beside him. He stopped for a red light, and when he put on the breaks the car skidded a bit on the wet pavement. The sack of groceries fell on him and a can of peas gouged him in the side. His first thought — *It's Dagger! I'm doomed!* Daddy remembered that can of harmless peas as he gave a friendly wave to the well dressed and very dangerous Dagger.

W. L. CRAWFORD

W. L. Crawford, unforgettable criminal lawyer, was known for his tears. He was able to cry on cue, and with those persuasive tears, he was able to turn any jury into a ball of putty ready for his molding. His wife was the first lady of art in the city. She turned their Ross Avenue home into a private art gallery. Thus, she was credited for introducing art to the Dallas public. Mrs. Crawford's collection of statuary and paintings reflected the taste of the era when she was a lady of consequence in Washington and Paris.

Before she married the judge, Mrs. Crawford was married to Lucius Quintus Cincinnatus Lamar II. This is a famous name in United States history. Lucius Quintus Cincinnatus I was a brilliant, fiery, influential Mississippi senator. He was included in John F. Kennedy's book, *Profiles in Courage.* Kennedy told of the day in 1874, when the freshman congressman, L. Q. C. Lamar from Mississippi, spoke ever so simply, yet ever so clearly, to touch the hearts of every listener as he pleaded for amity and justice between the North and the South. The U.S. Congress was still torn assunder by the remembrances of the war and with this one unforgettable speech, L. Q. C. Lamar reached some hearts and changed some attitudes of both Southerners and Northerners when he quoted his arch enemy, Charles Sumner of Massachusetts. "My countrymen — know one another, and you will love one another." Somehow after that day in 1874, the iron walls and the bitter fences that were still standing between the South and the North began to melt and fall.

This great man's son was also a statesman. When this son died, his widow came to Dallas with her little son, L. Q. C. Lamar III, and this lady married Judge Crawford. This son graduated from Dallas High School in 1899 and became — what else? — an attorney.

DON JANUARY AND THE 5TH HOLE

In 1923, the Dallas Park Board accepted a large plot of ground as a memorial. Walter A. Stevens and his sister, Annie L. Stevens, donated 40 acres in Oak Cliff in memory of their parents, Dr. and Mrs. John H. Stevens. The Park Commissioners purchased several adjoining tracts to the land, making the whole park 130 acres. A golf course was developed with a club house that opened May 17, 1924. The rolling hills and the woods made the course outstanding. There was one problem. Golf was still a new sport to the average Dallasite. The game belonged to the rich in private clubs, so the Park Department lost money the first four years that the course operated. However, by 1928, the course began not only to pay its way but also to make a profit. In the 30s, WPA funds kept the greens in perfect condition. In 1942, a new club house was built for $26,000, again with WPA funds.

About this time a young golfer, Don January was starting his career. Don, who has become a very successful professional golfer, is married to my college roommate, Pat. We've all been friends since college days. Don was telling me that when he was just starting out as a golfer, his father bought him a membership at Stevens Golf Course. Don remembered, "The cost was probably about $8, but I had my own locker. I could keep my things right there at the club. That made me feel like I had it made." Perhaps it was that locker plus talent that truly launched the winning career for Don. Nevertheless, the more Don played, the more balls he lost. Playing the 5th hole presented a real hazard. The balls continually went into the

147

water. Once, while Don was fishing for his ball in the water, he found not only his ball, but also many other balls. The 5th hole — it was a natural trap for balls. Don being an ingenious golfer in need of more balls, hollowed out a larger trap under the water. Not one ball that went into the water could escape the Don January trap. From then on, he always had plenty of balls!

CHAPTER VII

Some Places to See
Some Things to Do

THE BELO MANSION

Colonel Alfred Horatio Belo, Confederate officer, founded the *Dallas Morning News* in 1885. He had been a newspaper man in Galveston but decided to come to Dallas. He brought with him a marvelous publisher, George B. Dealey, to do the actual work at the paper. The Dealey family is still publishing the *Dallas Morning News* today.

In 1889, Belo hired Herbert Green, architect, to plan a home that would match the Belo home in Salem, North Carolina. The architect did just this. The Southern mansion stands on Ross at Pearl.

In 1926, the Sparkman family rented the building and converted it into a funeral home. By the way, the body of Clyde Barrow laid in state at this home. The Sparkmans managed their business in this place until 1973. The mansion was then totally renovated, and it is now owned by the Dallas Bar Foundation. It's a private club for attorneys.

THE DALLAS ZOO

The Dallas Zoo began in the City Park in 1884, moved to Fair Park in 1910, and then in 1912, it moved to the present site on a hill by the Trinity River. The area was once owned by T. L. Marsalis, but when Mr. Marsalis lost his fortune in the Depression of 1893, the property went to the city. "Bring 'Em Back Alive" Frank Buck, the big game hunter, furnished the zoo in the early days with many exotic animals.

I remember the zoo so well in the 1930s and 40s, because the city staged elaborate birthday parties for the elephants. Hundreds of school children turned out each year for the birthdays of Queenie and Wilbur, two particular favorites. I remember both elephants well, and I never missed a party. There was also Tootsie, Queenie's other child, who had great birthday celebrations. In fact, when Tootsie was five years old, in 1942, the *Dallas Times Herald* covered her party.

In order to attend Tootsie's party each kid had to bring scrap iron and rubber, so with one elephant bash, a lot of vital materials were collected for the war effort. Walton Carlton, zoo director in 1942, offered a giant ration stamp for the sugar in Tootie's cake.

Also in the 30s major changes occurred in the zoo when WPA funds were given to build better housing for the animals — nothing elaborate, however. Unfortunately, the layout of the park was not good, to say the least. Two streets ran through it, so cars were able to pass the monkeys on one side and the lions on the other, laying the park wide open to vandalism. Animals were shot and even poisoned. The *Dallas Time Herald,* so alarmed over all of this, offered a $1,000 reward for the apprehension of the vandal who poisoned Doug, a young chimpanzee. Eventually, the city council made it illegal to carry firearms on park property, but sill the problem existed.

After World War II, there was a bond program which included money to develop the zoo. This brought about criticism from the public because of the housing shortage that existed. "You've got pastures for the zebras, islands for the monkeys, and you've got houses for the lions — but not a dime for G.I. housing." Eventually, the Oak Cliff Exchange Club offered to create a long range continuous program of improvements for the zoo. The club established a fund made up of contributions from interested persons. The Dallas Zoological Society, which had been dropped for a number of years, was reorganized.

Hare and Hare planned a better zoo with pens surrounded by moats, giving better protection to the visitors and better care for the animals. Landscaping was included in this plan.

Further development brought the nation's first "miniature zoo." It was designed in small scale and allowed the children to come into contact with the baby animals. More improvements came in the 1960s. The Oak Cliff Lions Club generously gave $5,000 for a waterfall within the bird and reptile house. Today, the Marsalis Zoo is ranked with the ten top zoos of the country, and the director, Warren Iliff, is working diligently to see that our zoo remains on top.

THE GREAT STATE FAIR OF TEXAS

The *Dallas Morning News* did a big spread on my mother when she attended her 90th fair. Unfortunately, this was the last one she was going to attend, but for 90 years she had a great time at the exhibits and on the midway. I love the fair, because Mother certainly did. She remembered one fair, 1902, in particular, because it rained the whole time. She hadn't won anything on the midway either, and this added to her disappointment. It was all very discouraging. Mother had one nickle left, and it was time to go home. "One last try at the 'Go Fishing' booth just might pay off," she thought. "Surely I could get one of those glittery prizes." Mother fished and the man enthusiastically said, "Oh, little girl, you've won! Here is your teeny, weeny doll!" Mother remembered, "Was it ever teeny!" Poor dear! She didn't get much from the fair that year, but for 90 years, she claimed she got a lot — total enjoyment.

My first recollection of the Fair was the grand and glorious Centennial. I remember going in the main gate and being hypnotized by the lights, the flags, and the rippling lagoon. I asked my daddy if I could run — run hard like kids do. He told me I could run to the first building, but there I had to wait for him and my mother to catch up. So I ran! I ran into the porticos and there I saw those giant murals. I was a kid that never liked anything that was bigger than it was supposed to be. So when I saw them, I went into hysterics. Daddy rushed up to me to see what had happened. I just stood there screaming. Daddy didn't know if I had hurt myself, if someone had hurt me, or if something had bitten me. Finally, with my eyes closed, I was able to point to the murals and to scream about those wild looking people in the murals. Those bigger than life paintings are gone, and even though I am a member of the Friends of Fair Park, I will not insist that they be restored. I still don't like things bigger than they are supposed to be even if it's art.

One year at the Fair I met the Hum-A-Tune Man. He sold a musical instrument into which one hummed to make the music. Actually, it was just one step up from comb and tissue paper. As part of his spiel he brought a kid on stage and had that kid demonstrate the Hum-A-Tune. "Even a kid can play this instrument," he assured the gaping public. He brought me up! Ham that I am, I was thrilled. He called me *Magnolia*. I kept insisting that my name was *Rose-Mary*. He kept calling me Magnolia. It was all part of a great act.

There was Children's Day and all the free food. There was High School day and the football games. But for me, one thing stood out and will always stand out at the Fair — Fletcher's Corny Dogs! Neil Fletcher gave us manna from heaven.

In the 30s and 40s, the only professional theatre in Dallas was in a tent on Haskell Avenue. The acting company was called the Madcap Players. This tent theatre troupe was directed by Neil Fletcher and his wife Minnie. They were assisted by Toby and Jeannie Gunn. Jackie Caldwell played the organ each evening before the curtain went up. The plays changed weekly, but the plots of those plays always remained the same. Neil played the handsome hero, and Minnie was the dumb blond, Jeannie was the beautiful girl, and Toby was the comic. Other characters were hired when needed. One of these added actors was Wayne Babb. Later Wayne Babb felt that he was able to run his own theatre, so he opened a tent show on Fort Worth Avenue to serve the Oak Cliff drama enthusiasts. One of his supporting players was Bob Bly, a photographer with the *Oak Cliff Tribune*. When one looks at the sophisticated theatre scene in Dallas today, it's hard to think that at one time all professional theatre was offered in a tent.

Regardless of the tent, I never missed a show. In fact, I was so inspired by Neil Fletcher and his acting company that I made up my mind then and there that I would major in theatre when I got to col-

152

lege. It was my ambition to grow up and be a Madcap Player. Unfortunately, air conditioning came along, Dallas grew into a cosmopolitan city, and the Madcaps folded their tent but never went away. Neil, having a deep rolling toned voice, did a lot of radio and later television work. Some years ago, I made a television commercial with Neil. What a thrill! I felt that one of my life long ambitions had come to pass. I acted with Neil Fletcher.

When the Madcap Players folded, the Fletcher family was strapped financially. Neil tried everything to make a buck, including cooking. One evening in his kitchen, he created the corny dog. He came up with a batter than would cling to the dog, would fry up to a tasty crispy covering, and would all hang on to a stick. In 1942, the Fletcher corny dog was introduced to the eating public. I was there. Neil in a chef's hat standing behind a counter in a booth was frying the delectable treat. A voice, obviously Neil's, was booming out from a speaker telling all that passed by to stop and savor this new cuisine. The aroma from the deep fry pulled people in too!

Neil is gone, but the corny dog and his beautiful memory lives on!

THE DALLAS SUMMER MUSICALS

In 1940, just before the start of World War II, the Dallas Summer Musicals gave their first production in the band shell, Fair Park. The company was then called the Starlight Operettas. All the front seats — the front rows were seats, not benches — were priced at $1.80. The middle section of benches were $1.20, and up on the top tier, one could see the show for 60¢. Hyman Charninsky conducted the orchestra and college kids studying voice and dance made up the chorus. The stars were well known musical comedy veterans, and the character parts went to refugees of vaudeville. All of the productions were very professionally done, and Dallas patrons poured in to see the musicals in spite of the war news, the heat waves, and the June bugs.

There was one famous performance involving a June bug and Nannette Fabrey. She was a young star just emerging then, singing her heart out, when suddenly a June bug flew down her dress. She became hysterical, and I don't blame her. Those Texas critters are harmless, but they are BIG! Eventually, the show went on. Nothing really could stop those shows unless the rain got too heavy. Because the seats were so hard, cushions were rented for 25¢. I remember many a time putting the cushion on my head when it started to rain. None of us ever wanted to leave. This was live theatre for Dallas, and we all appreciated it so very much.

Mr. Tom Hughes, who presently is the producer of the Dallas Summer Musicals, loves to tell of those outdoor disturbances in the grand old days. There were the screams from the roller coaster riders that came during the tenor's high C. I remember those screams, but I never thought of them as being so disturbing or as funny as the Coke bottle that would roll from the top tiers on down to the orchestra pit. The audience would listen for the bottle to start its roll, gain momentum, and finally find a resting place in the $1.80 section.

Well, when air conditioning took over, the musicals moved inside and were billed as the State Fair Musicals, later to be the Dallas Summer Musicals. The shows moved into the auditorium that was built in 1925. The musicals, the symphony, the opera, the ballet, and the road shows continued to be given in this building. The hall served and served and served the arts, but finally in the early 70s, the city decided to completely renovate the grand old auditorium.

In the summer of 1973, the doors of a totally renovated music hall opened and John Davidson came to star in *Oklahoma*. Mr. Hughes, a college buddy of mine, invited me to play Aunt Eller in that production — a great moment in my life. As always, college music and dance students made up the singing chorus and dancing ensemble. Supporting roles were cast in New York or here in Dallas. The star came in and the whole show was put together in a week. Most of the supporting players had done their roles many times before, so it was just a matter of putting it all together. I had done Aunt Eller in the dinner theatres, so I was well prepared to once again sit at the churn and let Curly (John Davidson) sing "Oh, What a Beautiful Morning" to me!

The next year, I was privileged to perform in *No No Nanette* with Ginger Rogers. Imagine, I was going to tap with Ginger. I'll never forget the scene back stage when Ginger's mother, Lela Rogers, knelt down at her daughter's feet to buckle the star's tap shoes. Ginger was 63 at the time and her mother was 86. Would you call this motherly love, motherly obsession, or motherly abuse? Nevertheless, Ginger always gave a long curtain speech at the end of each performance. She was out front, the supporting characters were lined up behind her, and the chorus was at the back. She always pointed to that back row and exclaimed, "Those are the stars of tomorrow." This left us, the supporting actors and actresses, the middle row, undefined. We always suspected that we were the has beens of today. Whatever — those were tremendous times!

The musicals are different today. In the first place, the shows are so big that they can't be produced in a week. Peter Wolfe doesn't have the sets in stock. Costumes are sometimes under copyright. Mr. Hughes brings in shows that are mounted in New York and are made to travel. It's different, but still, the Dallas Summer Musicals are fabulous.

SYMPHONIES

My mother vaguely remembered attending the first Dallas Symphony concert which was given, May 22, 1900, at Turner Hall, corner of Harwood and Young. Hans Kreissig conducted. He was a very cultured young German musician who was conducting a musical group that ran into financial difficulties and got stranded in Texas. Since he was in the area, Kreissig decided to make Dallas his home, and since he needed work, he organized a symphony. This symphony orchestra consisted of anyone that he could find to play. He also gave piano lessons in order to make ends meet. Immediately, Mr. Kreissig involved a couple of Dallas society ladies in the project, and they became a great help to the symphony financially. Mrs. W. H. Abrams and Mrs. Jules Schneider organized the Symphony Club to help raise funds. There were eventually 21 violins in the group and the season consisted of three concerts.

Later in 1905, there was another attempt to organize a larger orchestra. This group was under the direction of Walter Fied, a German who came to Dallas to teach violin. Later, Carl Venth, who was concertmaster of the Metropolitan Opera and the Brooklyn Symphony, arrived in Dallas, so Fried gave the leadership of the symphony to Venth. Nevertheless, the real step forward for the Dallas Symphony came when Dr. Paul Van Katwijk, head of the music department at SMU, took up the baton. He performed wonders with the group.

As a kid, I remember going to the State Fair Music Hall to hear the symphony. *Peter and the Wolf* was always on the program. Marion Flagg, Music Director of the Dallas Schools, made certain that the school kids got, not just a sip, but a big gulp of symphonic music.

Besides those youth concerts, I got private concerts at home. Living the second door from me was a maiden lady, Miss Carrie Wheat, who took in roomers. During the depression this was not an unusual thing to do. Well, she had this roomer — a violinist in the Dallas Symphony. He made such little money that often he couldn't pay his room rent, so he would sit out on the front porch and play his violin. This brought out all the neighbors. We didn't have air conditioning in those days. All the doors and windows were open, so on hot summer nights we'd wait to hear the mellow sound from the violin and rush over to Miss Wheat's front porch. There we'd enjoy our private concert. Miss Wheat, of course, loved it. Being an old maid and alone a lot of the time, she really preferred the music and the company to the room rent.

Nevertheless, Jacques Singer was the conductor of the symphony in the 30s and he led the orchestra until 1942, when the symphony was disbanded because of World War II. Many years later, 1956, to be exact, my husband, Jack, and I met Mr. Singer in South Texas where he was conducting the Corpus Christi Symphony. Jack auditioned as timpanist with the orchestra. I went to that audition holding my kids, one on each hand, rushed up to Mr. Singer and exclaimed, "Oh, Mr. Singer, it's so wonderful to see you. I remember as a small child I went to all the concerts that you conducted in Dallas." With that one statement, I made him much older than he wanted to be. Nevertheless, Jack got the job.

In 1945, Antal Dorati revived the Dallas Symphony, and then, when I was in college, I remember enjoying the symphony under the leadership of Walter Hendl. There have been other conductors building up to the renowned, Eduardo Mata, who today is privileged to conduct the orchestra in the magnificent Morton H. Meyerson Symphony Hall. The hall was designed by I. M. Pei and it was named for an associate of Mr. Ross Perot.

My husband, Jack, today is timpanist for the Fort Worth

Symphony Orchestra. Brooks Morris, a fine musician organized the symphony in Fort Worth in 1912. The orchestra gave concerts until it was forced to disband during World War I when there simply were no musicians available to play. Then in the spring of 1925, Brooks Morris went to society and amusement editor of the Fort Worth Record, Lela Rogers, and said, "I think it is about time Fort Worth had a symphony again. I'm not willing to raise my children in a city which doesn't have a symphony orchestra." So from the Musician's Union, Texas Hotel Orchestra, Texas Christian University Music Department, Burns School of Music, Majestic Theatre and Palace Theatre Orchestra, Montgomery Ward Orchestra, Baptist Seminary Music Department, Meadows School of Music, and Rosenthal School of Music, Morris collected 68 musicians to play that first concert, December 11, 1925. The concert was presented in the First Baptist Church auditorium, 4,000 patrons attending. Over 300 people had to be turned away.

Society editor, Lela Rogers, became the business manager, publicity director, and chief fund raiser for the first few months. With the money she earned she was able to buy the costumes for her daughter who had just won a Charleston contest and was bound for Broadway/Hollywood. The daughter — Ginger Rogers. Brooks Morris was the conductor until 1962.

In 1972, a Fort Worth musician, with music degrees from TCU, mounted the podium and became an extremely popular conductor, Mr. John Giordano. The smyphony surged ahead. Giordano created the Fort Worth Chamber Orchestra, a small group that tours all over the state. This group in 1980, was asked to play at Carnegie Hall for the opening of a chamber orchestra series that the famed hall was sponsoring. (As the old joke would imply, this group must have practiced.) The chamber orchestra toured Mexico, Spain, and China, playing a concert on The Great Wall. A real "feather in the cap" comes to the Fort Worth Symphony every four years when the orchestra hosts the Van Cliburn Piano Competition.

Many other symphonies exist in the area — Richardson, Garland, Irving, and Mesquite, all have orchestras. Plano and Dallas have excellent chamber groups. All of these performing artists are supported by the community.

OLD CITY PARK

As a child, my mother played in the Old City Park, but at the turn of the century when she was doing her playing, the park was not *Old* City Park, it was *The* City Park. It was *the* park for downtown kids. The park was established in 1876, so in 1976, it became a grand scene of celebration, and truly, there was a lot to celebrate. In 1976, the nation was 200 years old, the park was 100 years old, and the Dallas Heritage Society had accomplished its goal.

In 1966, the Dallas Heritage Society raised $30,000 to save Millermore, the mansion built by Dallas pioneer, William Brown Miller. Mr. Miller brought his family and his slaves to Dallas in the 1850s. He acquired land out on what is Bonnie View Road, and with slave labor built his grand mansion which he called Millermore. Some person of the Miller family lived in the house until 1966, when the last Miller girl died. In typical Southern tradition, the house was crumbling around this maiden lady who was determined to stay in the old homestead until it collapsed. Well, it almost did. After her death, it looked like the bulldozer was going to take over. But — HARK! — enter the Dallas Heritage Society. This organization of interested Dallas citizens got the money together to save the building. It was dismantled and the boards were carefully numbered, so, not like Humpty-Dumpty, it could be put back together again. The house was rebuilt in the Old City Park, and this majestic mansion became the nucleus of a whole bunch of structures that were going to be restored and moved into the park. Today, there is a doctor's office, a Victorian house, two general stores, a bank, a lawyer's office, a print shop, a church, a gazebo, the railway station, and many other buildings that make up this 19th century town. It's a walking museum, and I can assure you that everyone loves it. I often take people who are in Dallas for a convention through the park, and regardless of the place these people call home, they still all love to stroll down Main Street, 1900. Thank God for the Dallas Heritage Society!

My good buddy Don Payton, who is a Research Associate with the Dallas Historical Society, traced his family through the slaves of William Brown Miller. Like Alex Haley, Don found his "Roots." Mr. Miller in 1865, not only freed his slaves, but also gave them land which various members of the Payton family still own. I've always appreciated Don, because he listened to his grandmother. He

158

has this marvelous presentation about his family and his family's relationship with the Millers. I've heard Don tell his grandmother's stories. All the other kids were running around senselessly, but not Don. He listened to every word Grandmother had to say, and now he knows a lot about his family and Dallas. He's a valuable member of the Dallas Historical Society. I feel that a person who gives an ear to the past, has a brighter eye on the future. Hey, that's profound. Someone ought to write it down!

ESTATES

At one time there were several large country estates within the bounds of Dallas County. No more! — unless you count J. R.'s spread out at Southfork, and this property is not in Dallas County. And too, J. R. has been cancelled.

Across the street from Northpark Shopping Center on Northwest Highway is the Caruth farm. The elegant farm house and the traditional barn can be seen from the parking lot of the shopping center. Mr. Caruth owned oil wells and other valuable land. This last farm in the city of Dallas is now being divided into lots that hold huge townhouses. Some of the Caruth land will go to the widening of North Central Expressway.

Captain Josey had a ranch in Carrollton, the remains of which are quite visible. The old barn still has Josey's picture painted on it.

In Oak Cliff, there was Villa Vista, a 30 acre estate owned by bridge builder Charles R. Moore. The estate extended from Kessler Parkway on over to Forth Worth Avenue. Interstate 30 runs right through the once peaceful haven. Charles Moore built a Dallas landmark — the Triple Underpass. The next time you choose Elm, Main, or Commerce, you might think of him. He also built the Commerce Street Viaduct, the one time Dallas Interurban Bridge, and the Galveston Causeway. In fact, his firm, the Austin Bridge Company, now located at 2949 Stemmons, has built bridges in all of the 254 counties in Texas.

In East Dallas, oil man Everett DeGolyer had a great estate on the east bank of White Rock Lake. He willed his in-town paradise to SMU, who in turn sold the land and house to the city. Now, this lovely piece of property with the next door Camp Estate is part of the Arboretum, enjoyed by all flower loving citizens.

My dear friend, Sue Herzog Johnson, was the private librarian for Everett DeGolyer. She officed at the masion and took care of his rare book collection. Through my friendship with Sue, I met Mr. DeGoyler one day and had a nice long chat with him. He shared this story with me and as far as I know, it's never been published.

In the early days of the Texas Republic, an argument arose. Who was the first Texas poet? Mirabeau Lamar, who served as the second president of the Republic of Texas, always claimed that he was the first Texas poet. However, there was a newspaper man, Hugh Kerr, who also claimed to be the first person in Texas to write poetry. The whole argument was rather silly. Today there are people up East who don't think people in Texas even read poetry much less write it. Nevertheless, the argument continued. Finally, when Lamar became completely exasperated with this poetic claim of Hugh Kerr, he wrote this little doggerel. "Kerr, Kerr, Kerr. What cha write them poems fer?"

THE HEARD MUSEUM

The Heard Natural Science Museum and Wildlife Sanctuary is a great place to spend a day. Miss Bessie Heard, daughter of a pioneer Collin County family and a native of McKinney collected shells, butterflies, nature prints, oriental art, cut glass, beautiful silver, rare pottery — actually everything. Soon her collections outgrew her house, so she contacted John Ripley Forbes of the Natural Science of Youth Foundation. He guided her to the establishment of the Bessie Heard Foundation in 1964. Her collections became a museum that can be enjoyed by all. There is so much more now. There are exotic animals and birds, alive and stuffed. There are nature trails through the large sanctuary. There are rocks to study, birds to watch, facts to gather. There's so much to do at the Heard Museum that I believe you had better spend two days at the least. I love the nature trails that wind through the woods and introduce the hiker to all sorts of unusual flora and fauna. There is a terrific museum store with really nifty things for any young nature lover — rocks, butterfly nets, arrow heads, etc.

Each year, my dear friend, Mrs. Mary Lee Heard, who laughingly claims that she is the last of the Heards, invites me to speak to the auxiliary of the museum. It's a grand affair held at the Heard auditorium in downtown McKinney. For years, Miss Bessie came to these luncheons, but she died a couple of years ago at the ripe old age of 101. Her legacy lives on.

CHAPTER VIII

Some Texas Personalities
With a Dallas Connection

MOLLIE BAILEY

My mother often spoke of going to the Mollie Bailey Show. Mollie presented the first circus in Texas. In the 1800s and early 1900s, she'd roll into Dallas, pitch her circus tents out at the Fair Park and invite the folks to see a very special show. Everyone loved Mollie, including my mother.

Very good friends of mine, Adelyn Hancock and Caroly Selzer, have a great story about their mother, Hallie Fannin, and the Mollie Bailey Show. Hallie was invited to go see Mollie by a young man in town, Porter Spikes. Hallie's mother wisely said, "I'd better give you a quarter in case he doesn't have one to pay your way into the circus." Mrs. Fannie remembered that when she and her young date arrived at the box office, Porter turned to her and said, "Give me your quarter, so I can pay your way into the circus." This story was printed in the Mabank *Texas Banner* in 1969. Porter Spikes, who lived in California at the time, read the story and sent Mrs. Fannin a quarter. This was almost 70 years after their date. Her daughters have the letter, and, of course, the cherished quarter.

Mollie Bailey was a colorful Texas character. She was born

162

Mollie Kirkland, 1841, in Alabama. One summer, while she was at home on vacation from a girl's finishing school in Tuscaloosa, she announced to her father, William Kirkland, that she was going to see the circus that was in town. Because a fine, finished Southern lady would never think of attending a circus, her father forbade her to go.

Mollie went anyway and instantly fell in love with the good-looking red-haired trumpet player in the circus, Gus Bailey. His parents owned the circus. Gus courted Mollie the brief time that the circus was in town, much to the dismay of her father. When the circus left, so did Mollie. Her father never spoke to her again even though the marriage was successful and she had eight children, the first of whom she named William Kirkland Bailey. Mollie wrote herself into the family act immediately, and she performed regularly when she wasn't having children.

When the Civil War began, Gus promptly enlisted in Hood's Brigade, a Texas Confederate troop. Mollie appointed herself a one-woman morale builder and entertained troops. She wrapped medicine in her hair and went through Yankee lines to minister to the wounded Confederates. She disguised herself as an old woman and talked herself through Northern lines, taking food to captured Southerners.

Gus tried to keep his spirit up as Mollie did, but he admitted that the South was doomed. He wrote the song, "The Old Gray Mare," to explain his feelings. The lyrics stated that the South, like the mare, "shore ain't what she used to be." Mollie wasn't easily defeated. She made the tune the marching song of the men, and they tramped through Texas singing it in double-time.

After the war, the Bailey family joined a showboat on the Mississippi River. Finally, there was enough money to buy a circus. The Mollie Bailey Show toured only Texas, but that was enough for Mollie. A TEXAS SHOW FOR TEXAS PEOPLE. She gave it her all. When she roared into a Texas town, the populace got the finest entertainment that could be had. Whenever the show came to town, the handbills passed out by the advance men to the townfolk simply stated, "Aunt Mollie is coming!"

Aunt Mollie had such an unforgettable and winning personality that it took only her name to sell tickets. She wore glistening diamonds on every finger, and she flashed a grin that made even the

163

stingiest miser buy at least one ticket. She'd bring smiles to the whole crowd when she'd yell out the platitude, "You can't take it with you, so buy a ticket." One truism was strictly her own: "If you're not enthusiastic about living — drop dead!"

Mollie retired to Houston when she was 75. Her children tried to run the show without her, but this turned out to be impossible. Mollie was the show.

MA FERGUSON

We have a woman governor, Ann Richards. However, Ann is not the first woman to serve as Governor of Texas. We had Ma Ferguson, who not only was the first woman governor of Texas, but she was also the first woman ever elected to a governorship in the United States.

Marian Amanda Wallace was born into a very wealthy family of Bell County. She had the initials M. A. W., so she was called Ma when she ran for public office. She was also called Ma, because she was married to Pa Ferguson. Her husband, Jim Ferguson, was elected governor in 1915 on the "Farmer's" ticket. Farmer Jim was another name Pa used. He wanted everyone to know that he was of rural stock. This was important to anyone running for an office in Texas in 1915, because the state was rural then. Pa assured all the farmers in Texas that they were his primary interest. He came out of the fields himself. He had worked his way through school. He was one of the gang. He was elected.

"Texans, there are three things you can believe in — God Almighty, the Sears and Roebuck Catalogue, and Jim Ferguson." That profound statement convinced the people of Texas that Jim was their man.

At first, he got along well with the legislature. Most of his programs for the farmers became laws. He issued free textbooks to the children and acquired funds for the improvement of rural schools. He faced Pancho Villa's Bandits on the border, and welcomed John J. Pershing and the National Guard Units into the area during this Mexican uprising.

At the Democratic Convention he spoke against prohibition and woman's suffrage. There were hisses from the balcony from the women present. It was rather ironic that he campaigned against the woman's vote, when his wife was soon to be governor.

Ferguson unfortunately got into a disagreement with the regents of the University of Texas over money and teaching staff. There were also other problems. He was paying personal bills with state funds. He was depositing state funds into banks which he owned giving no interest to the state. He got money from sources he refused to identify. In other words, Pa was stealing everything in Texas that wasn't nailed down.

So, in 1917, he was impeached, and Lieutenant Governor Bill Hobby, Sr. then became governor. Hobby vowed he'd fight "Fergusonism" all the way. Hobby and his constituents lost the battle, because in 1925, Pa ran Ma, and she won.

"Well, we have returned. We departed in disgrace; we now return in glory," Ma shouted. She had campaigned with this promise, "Two governors for the price of one." She fought against the Ku Klux Klan, which was a major issue at that time. She fought against bilingual education. "If the English language was good enough for Jesus Christ, it's good enough for the children of Texas," was one of Ma's observations.

My mother remembered Ma Ferguson campaigning in Oak Cliff. The crowds assembled on either side of Jefferson Boulevard, and Ma passed by in a touring car waving and smiling to the mob. The crowd responded with a hearty "Turkey Pan!" That's what everyone shouted to Ma — Turkey Pan. There was no reasoning behind the cry, except for the fact that Ma was rural, and I guess turkey pans go with rural life. Who knows?

Ma won again in 1933. After she served this term, she opened the doors of the Huntsville State Prison, and let everyone out. My daddy said the joke of the day was in the response one would give when someone made a mistake. "Oh, pardon me," one would apologize. The response was, "Well, Ma Ferguson would." There was real controversy over those pardons. Many people said, "Don't you talk about Ma Ferguson. My Papa got to come home."

Ma ran again in 1939, but she lost to a man more rural than she was — Willard Lee O'Daniel. Fergusonism was finally out of Texas politics.

Ma lived until 1961, when Lyndon Johnson came to her bedside and sang her campaign song to her, "Put On Your Old Gray Bonnet." This finished her off. She is buried in the State Cemetery, and her tomb reads:

Life's Race Well Run
Life's Work Well Done
Life's Victory Won
Now Cometh Rest.

GAIL BORDEN

As a child and even now I have always had a special love for
Elsie, the Borden Milk Cow. She had two things that I yearned for
as a kid — big brown eyes and a skirted vanity. When I was about
ten years old, the rage of the day for little girls was a dressing table
(vanity) with a skirt around it. A little girl really had it made if the
skirt material matched the bed spread and the curtains in her room.
A really cool Bobby Soxer could not live without a skirt dresser.
Well, I didn't have one, and I really didn't think I was living. I was
disgusted about it, and then my disgust turned to anger when I realized that Elsie the Cow had a skirt dresser. During the State Fair
in the 30s and 40s, the Old Mill Restaurant was operated by the
Borden Milk Company. At the fair, Elsie was always housed there
to greet her fans. Fair goers were allowed to go into her boudoir. I
was about ten years old when I walked into Elsie's bedroom. There
it was — a skirted vanity. Of course, it was cow size. She had a bed
spread and curtains to match — all cow size. Her big brown eyes
looked at me in a rather smug fashion. She was a cool cow and I was
a nobody. I turned to my mother. "Even that cow has a skirt
dresser." I remember that when Christmas came that year, I got a
skirt dresser.

Some of you might not know that Elsie, that Borden Cow, is a
Texan. Here's the story. The year was 1839. Gail Borden, Jr. had
been in Texas for ten years, and he considered himself a failure. He
often asked himself, "Where have your dreams brought you?" His
answer was always the same, "Nowhere!" To console himself a bit
he thought, "You are nearly forty and your flint is hardly scratched.
You must learn patience. Impatience comes easy to men who would
set the world ablaze."

The members of the Borden family were star gazers and trail
blazers. The first Bordens in America were followers of the liberal
Baptist, Roger Williams, who fled from the strict Puritanical laws
and set up his Baptist Church in Providence, Rhode Island, 1638.

There had been five generations of Bordens in America and the sixth, Gail Borden, Jr., was born November 9, 1801, in the frontier town, Norwich, New York. The little boy grew up knowing the Indians, the forests, the wilderness, and having the desire to go out and conquer the land. His father had the urge of the early explorers when he took his family down the Ohio River to settle in Kentucky, land of blue grass and tobacco. Gail Borden, Sr. helped in the founding of Covington, Kentucky, a city named after one of the heroes of the War of 1812. Son Gail grew up aware that Andy Jackson showed John Bull how Western men could fight, and the British decided that they didn't want any of it. A great spirit was in the little boy.

At the age of twenty-two Gail, Jr. went down the Mississippi River and settled in Amite County, Mississippi State, and there he began to teach school. He met a lot of members of the prominent, Baptist Mercer family, and he married the prettiest member of all, Penelope. The fever of adventure in Texas was fanned by Stephen Fuller Austin, and Gail and his wife decided to go to the new territory. They had to hurry, because Penelope was just about to deliver their first child. The baby, a girl, was born on Galveston Island, December 24, 1829.

In order to support his family, Gail took up farming, stock raising, and surveying. Lots of surveyors were needed, because Texas was large and only 2,000 people were in the territory at the time. Now, these people who were settling in Texas were not against the control of the Mexican government, but the arrogant power displayed by Santa Anna did make the new Texans think about independence and a free republic.

A meeting was held at San Felipe, October 1, 1832. In that delegation was Gail Borden, James Bowie, David G. Burnet, Sam Houston, and the central figure, Stephen F. Austin. Austin was the spirit of Texas, and it was then that Gail Borden decided that he would be the voice of Texas. He acquired a press and began to publish the *Telegraph and Texas Register*. This was the tenth newspaper that was started in Texas and it was the only one that lasted two years. The first edition was published October 10, 1835. There were no thundering editorials. It was only a small journal of eight pages of news. Borden had no ax to grind, only news to report. However, when the seige of the Alamo which began February 23,

1836, ended in defeat for the Texans, Borden with pride published the Texas Declaration of Independence for Sam Houston. There were stories of Santa Anna's pitching the press into the Gulf and of Borden fishing it out to continue printing the news of declared freedom.

When Texas did become a republic, Borden became a customs collector in Galveston. The island was booming in trade. However, Borden felt unfulfilled. This is when he looked at himself — ten years in Texas and he was still just a "tinkerer." He had tinkered in teaching, farming, stock raising, printing, and surveying. He threw himself into the building of the city of Galveston and of the First Baptist Church there. Later some of his customs collecting procedures were questioned, so he left that job. Then his beloved wife, Penelope, died. Now, he was extremely depressed over his life.

When he was fifty years old, he heard of the 49ers leaving for California. It was always the same story with the pioneers. If the food held out, they'd make it to their destination. If there wasn't enough food, they'd die. Borden began to work with a meat biscuit that wouldn't go rancid on the trail. It was a condensed form of meat that would last even in hot weather. He worked diligently on this biscuit. It was advertised all over the country. The biscuit even went to the Crimean War where the famed nurse, Florence Nightingale, had a bite.

He got little money from his biscuit, but what he did get he used to work with condensing milk. Housewives boiled fruit and the jelly from the boiling would keep for some time. Would milk do the same? Could one preserve milk? Borden condensed his milk, and the milk still had quality taste. It was a miracle. Scientists had never been able to do what the Texas tinkerer had done. Patent #15,553, condensing milk in vacuum over low heat, came to be the vast food processing company we know today, the Borden Milk Company.

Borden always remained popular around the First Baptist Church Galveston. He said to his minister, James Huckins, "I've condensed milk. You do it to your sermons." It was Rufus C. Burleson, then pastor of the First Baptist Church, Houston, later President of Baylor University, who said, "Gail Borden was so filled with the milk of human kindness, he just had to invent condensed milk."

168

CHAPTER IX

Some Thoughts

THE FUTURE

Obviously, I was reared to love Dallas, so I wish for my city only the best. First and foremost, I pray for unity, particularly, racial unity. This book is my story of Dallas, so it's definitely a "white man's" story. I pray that in the next 150 years, the metroplex will grow and develop with many black businesses. Recently, Dallas Baptist University gave me the Good Samaritan Award. I shared this award with Comer J. Cottrell, a black business man known for his charitable and philanthropic efforts for education. Mr. Cottrell was responsible for the moving of Paul Quinn College from Waco to Dallas. It is now on the campus of Bishop College. Mr. Cottrell started Pro-Line Corporation in 1970 with $600 and a borrowed typewriter. Today, his company, which makes and sells cosmetics for black people, is the largest black-owned business in the Southwest.

Alan Young, owner of Alan Young Buick-GMC began operating his dealership in Northeast Tarrant County as part of the General Motors Corporation's minority dealer development program in 1985.

In the Industrial-Service listings, Drew Pearson Enterprises Inc. ranks in the nation at 82. His company deals in sports licensing and sportswear manufacturing.

This is a strong start for black businesses in the area. May there be more.

I pray that downtown Dallas will be revitalized. This is so important if the city wants to continue attracting conventions to the area.

I pray that something will be done with the Trinity River. This project has been on the drawing board for over 100 years. Could something be done soon?

THE END

My Grandpa Hass did own and operate one of the first and finest bakeries in Dallas, but his business came to an abrupt end on October 24, 1929, the day the stock market crashed. It was all over for him. He saw no hope of regaining what he had had, and obviously he felt that he couldn't live without the business and the money, so he jumped from the Commerce Street viaduct to his death on April 9, 1930. The headline in the *Dallas Morning News* read "Despondent Businessman Leaps to Death." My daddy in an interview stated that Mr. Hass had been depressed since the first of the year when the business closed. In my grandfather's pocket was a list of grocers that he was planning to see just in case one of them wanted to finance a bakery. Evidently, there was no one who could do this. The country was in a deep depression. In fact, the whole world was in a financial slump to end all slumps.

My daddy with his great sense of humor and my mother, who was not only funny, but a little zany as well, struggled on in spite of all. On September 14, 1932, at Baylor Hospital, a little ray of sunlight came into their lives — ME! I grew up with very little but didn't know it. The family estate that had fallen like the stock market, now consisted of a few pieces of cut glass and a few pieces of jewelry. But I got several things worth millions. First and foremost, I got a lot of love and encouragement. With love in her voice my mother would scream, "Get an education. They can't take that away from you." So I went to school and studied hard.

Then, of course, I got the family stories — what treasures! My daddy died in 1968. He was *still* working. After you pass 50 you go into the STILL generation. No one will ever ask how you are doing. They will ask if you're *still* working, *still* driving, or *still* living in your home. That last question use to infuriate my mother. "Are you *still* in your home?" She'd snap back with, "Of course, where do you think I'd be?"

Well, nevertheless, daddy became very ill, but fortunately he was not ill very long before he died. We called it a "blessing," and it was. Daddy wrote me a letter before he died. In the first paragraph, he willed me my mother. I didn't mind that. I had a lot of fun taking care of her. In the second paragraph he told me how to settle his business affairs. To me, this was harder to do than the taking care of my mother. Ah, but then he concluded his letter. "Let there be no long mourning for me, for I will be with my Lord." He signed his name. That's called FAITH!

Well, I took care of Mother until she died in 1983. She was not ill long — another blessing. I did marvelous things for my mother in front of my children. Let's hope they go out and do likewise.

And, here I am. People come up and ask me every day, "Are you STILL here?"

Here's Madame Sarah Bernhardt holding her dog. She's out at Fair Park with her tent pitched near the railroad tracks. Note the French flag and the American flag blowing in the breeze. Note the English writing and the French writing. My dear friend, Bill Overton, Professor of Drama, Abilene, Texas, secured this picture for me.

My mother, the flapper, standing in front of the family treasure, a car!

My daddy, the Doughboy, in France, 1917. After the war he settled in Dallas rather than returning to the family spread in South Texas. After all, How ya gonna keep 'em down on the farm after they've seen Paree? (The word doughboy was used, because during the Civil War, the brass buttons on the infantry uniforms looked like the globular biscuits that were served to sailors in 1770. Eventually, the name was laid upon the soldiers themselves.)

Here are my great-grandparents, the Balitzs. They wandered to Dallas after the Civil War. I do believe they have a look of the "old country" about them!

The house on West 10th. Standing on the porch are my mother, grandmother, and aunt. Aunt Katie wasn't a woman yet — short skirt!

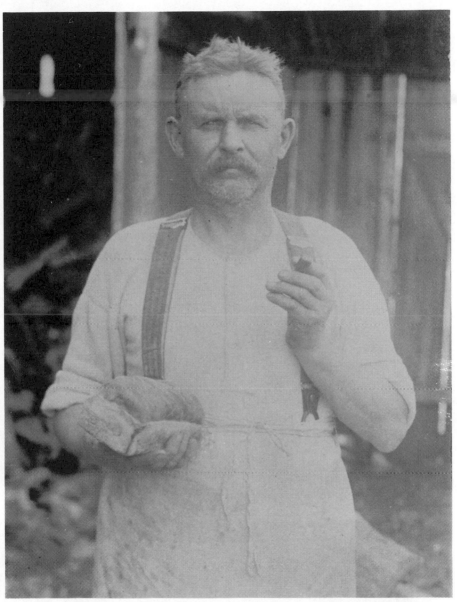

My grandfather with his two favorite possessions — a loaf of bread and a good cigar.

The bakers and the children are taking a breather. This building on Main Street was torn down to build the Kennedy Memorial.

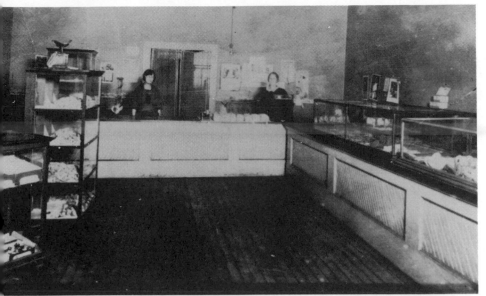

Here's the bakery, inside view. That's my aunt and grandmother behind the counter.

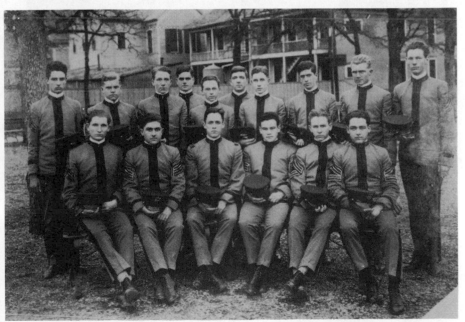

The first ROTC unit at Dallas High on Bryan Street. The Plaza of the Americas is standing now where these guys were standing in 1916. My dear friend, Thelma Maas, gave this picture to me. Her husband was in the corps.

Tootsie's birthday party. Director of the zoo, Walton Carlton, is holding a giant ration stamp to cover the sugar in Tootsie's cake.

A kindergarten class has a May Pole Celebration in Old City Park, 1900.
That's Harwood Street in the background. My dear friend, Margaret
Claypool's mother Mamie Slaughter, the teacher, is on the right. Mrs.
Keller, head of the kindergarten, is on the left. Lucile Harwood is the
child on the far right and Rena Munger is the child on the far left. Caro-
line Candler is in the center. She was of the Candler's of Atlanta, owner of
Coca-Cola.

My girl scout troop in back of Robert E. Lee Elementary School. That tree still stands on Matilda Street between Vanderbilt and Goodwin. Left to right are Nita Carol Cervin (married French royalty), Betsy Lou Jeter Gano (Mrs. Jeter was a troop leader), unidentified friend, Billye Faye Maples, Marcy Jo Swindel, and me.

The branch bakery, 439 S. Lamar. My mother and her sister with old Shep are on the porch.